FAVRE

THE MAN · THE LEGEND

Jeffrey Phelps; following spread: David Joles

MILWAUKEE · WISCONSIN
JOURNAL SENTINEL
jsonline.com

TRIUMPH
BOOKS

Packers quarterback Brett Favre celebrates a four-yard, first-quarter Ahman Green rushing touchdown during the Packers 40-34 overtime loss to the Kansas City Chiefs, Sunday, Oct. 12, 2003, at Lambeau Field in Green Bay.

Content packaged by Milwaukee Journal Sentinel and Mojo Media, Inc.

Milwaukee Journal Sentinel
Project Coordination and Design: Bob Friday
Book Photo Editor: Mark Hoffman
Photo Technician: Jack Emmrich
Graphics: Louis K. Saldivar, Enrique Rodriguez
Assistant Sports Editor/Copyeditor: Louisa Boardman
Photo Editor: Sherman Williams
Sports Editor: Garry D. Howard
Marketing: Thomas Baylerian, David Wise

Mojo Media, Inc.
Editor: Joe Funk
Creative Director: Jason Hinman

Parts of this book are excerpted from a series published in the Milwaukee Journal Sentinel in 2005.

This book is available in quantity at special discounts for your group
or organization. For further information, contact:

Triumph Books
542 South Dearborn Street
Suite 750
Chicago, Illinois 60605
(312) 939-3330
Fax (312) 663-3557

Printed in United States of America
ISBN: 978-1-57243-920-7

Rick Wood

Table of Contents

Ever the improviser, Green Bay Packers quarterback Brett Favre releases a shovel pass to Dorsey Levens for a first down while in the grasp of Carolina Panthers linebacker Kevin Greene during the third quarter of the 1996 season NFC Championship Game. The 30-13 victory over the Panthers on Jan. 12, 1997, at Lambeau Field in Green Bay sent the Packers to the Super Bowl.

Jeffrey Phelps

FOREWORD
Brett Favre: The Man, The Legend
Garry D. Howard • Assistant Managing Editor/Sports • Milwaukee Journal Sentinel

Through two decades, Green Bay Packers fans had waited for a worthy successor to Bart Starr. They longed for a quarterback who would lead their storied team back to where it belonged, on top of the National Football League.

Like Starr, who led the Packers to five NFL championships in the 1960s, the quarterback they'd been waiting for came out of the Deep South – a youngster with a cannon for an arm, acquired (some would say stolen) from Atlanta for a first-round draft pick in 1992 by general manager Ron Wolf.

He wasn't very polished, at least not at first.

But he was "must-see TV," from his first home appearance that September, when he replaced an injured Don Majkowski and rallied the team to a victory over the Cincinnati Bengals.

And he was the Packers' starting quarterback in every game after that until his retirement in March 2008.

There was the steady rise of the team back to respectability. There was the signing of free-agent defensive end Reggie White, perhaps the best ever to play his position, who had been drawn to Favre's toughness after separating the young quarterback's shoulder on a sack but failing to knock him out of the game.

There were the three consecutive MVP awards from 1995 to 1997 – an NFL record. There were the two National Football Conference championships in 1996 and 1997. There was, of course, the Super Bowl XXXI victory over the New England Patriots to cap the '96 season and return the Lombardi Trophy to Green Bay.

There were the 253 consecutive regular-season starts, shattering the record for his position; the 442 touchdown passes, 61,655 passing yards and 160 victories.

Then there was that "aw-shucks" approach to life that endeared him even more to Packers fans.

How do you adequately cover such a career?

You start with some of the best football beat writers in the business, led by Bob McGinn and Tom Silverstein, who were there for every single snap Favre took under center.

As No. 4 began to consider retirement in the later years of his career, the sports staff of the Milwaukee Journal Sentinel crafted a season-long series examining Favre's life and career in 17 chapters. Assistant Sports Editor Louisa Boardman laid out the roadmap.

McGinn, Silverstein, Gary D'Amato and Lori Nickel provided in-depth reporting and insightful writing. Our award-winning photography staff, led by assistant managing editor Sherman Williams, documented Favre's stellar career with one striking photograph after another.

It's all here. His childhood in Kiln, Mississippi; playing high school ball under his father and coach (who didn't like to pass); his college career at Southern Mississippi, which was barely interrupted by a near-fatal car accident; his wild rookie season as a benchwarmer in Atlanta; his rise with the Packers to become one of the greatest and most popular players in pro football history; his addiction to painkillers; his growing maturity; his legendary toughness.

We set out to produce a book worthy of the man it covers. I hope you enjoy it. ❹

RAISED ON GRIT

Favre was toughened by brothers, dad

By Gary D'Amato

Fenton, Miss. – Every legend has a beginning, and the legend of Brett Favre began right here, in the backwoods of southern Mississippi, on 52 ½ acres of pine trees and meadows tucked between Mill Creek and the Rotten Bayou.

Ravaged in 2005 by Hurricane Katrina, the Favre homestead was, in the 1970s and '80s, the ideal place for three rough-and-tumble sons of a high school football coach to play their games.

Scott, Brett and Jeff Favre, inseparable by blood and isolated by geography, could fish and swim in the bayou, hunt in the woods and play football and baseball on makeshift fields between barns and outbuildings.

"We didn't grow up in a subdivision or a populated area, where you have neighbors right next to you," said Jeff Favre, the youngest brother and the third of Irvin and Bonita's four children. "We couldn't call buddies and meet up in a park or field and in 15 minutes you've got some game. That was not available to us, so we played with each other."

They were always throwing something, those Favre boys. Rocks, potatoes, balls made from rolled-up wads of duct tape, whatever else was handy. They were always competing, too, their spirited games sometimes ending with one brother wrestling in the mud with another.

"There wasn't no sissies around here," said David Peterson, a cousin whom the Favres treated like a fourth brother. "We used to go in that old barn and everybody would hide and we'd throw rocks at each other and see if we could knock each other out. I tell you what, I don't know how Aunt Bonita and them made it with us. Whew! We was wild.

"It's probably a good thing we didn't live in the city because we would have tore things up."

In the evenings, they'd come tumbling into the modest ranch house, dirty and bleeding from this cut or that scrape, laughing and bragging and needling each other about home runs and touchdowns and game-saving tackles.

Bonita invariably had a pot of something going on the stove.

"God, did they eat," she said. "You put it there, buddy, they ate it."

They were good athletes, too; strong, raw-boned boys who always threw harder, swung harder, tackled harder and played harder than the other kids in Pee Wee football and Little League baseball.

"We were always better than everybody else," said

Favre horses around with his dad and former Packer Esera Tuaolo in 1993 at the Favre family home near Kiln, Miss.

"That was Irv's patented move right there. Broken leg? Put some ice on it, you'll be all right. Get back out there."

Steve Haas,
owner of Broke Spoke bar in Kiln, Miss.,
on Brett's dad as a coach

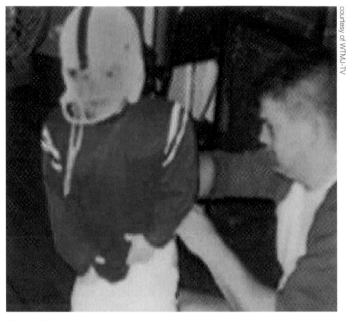

courtesy of WTMJ-TV

Brett Favre gets help from his dad, Irvin, as he puts on his first football uniform at Christmas 1970.

Scott Favre, not so much bragging as stating a fact.

Brett, the middle son, weighed 9 pounds 15 ounces when he was born on Oct. 10, 1969.

"The doctor said he was ready for a hamburger," Bonita said.

He was preordained by genetics to grow into a strapping 6-foot-2, 230-pound man. He was nurtured in an environment of intense competition with his brothers and extended family members. He soaked up the lessons taught by his late father, a widely admired and hard-nosed coach.

But could anyone around Kiln, the one-stoplight town nearby, have predicted that Brett Favre would one day rank among the greatest quarterbacks in National Football League history?

Could anyone have predicted that he would be a three-time league MVP who would lead the Green Bay Packers to victory in Super Bowl XXXI?

Could anyone have predicted that in 17 seasons of pro football he would rack up 253 consecutive starts, an NFL record for quarterbacks?

"No way," said Rocky Gaudin, who coached Brett from the fifth grade on and was an assistant coach under Irv at Hancock North Central High School. "I told him when he came through that he was the best quarterback we ever had at that time as far as being a competitor and a good leader.

"But he was not necessarily the best quarterback we'd had in terms of his accuracy. Even though we didn't throw much, he was pretty erratic."

Not even his brothers pegged him as a future NFL quarterback, let alone a surefire first-ballot Hall of Famer.

"It wasn't that early that I could sit here and say, 'He's going to be a professional football player,'" said Scott Favre, who was regarded by some as the better quarterback prospect of the two.

The truth was, Brett probably was a better high school baseball player than he was a football player. He started for Hancock North Central as an eighth-grader and earned five varsity letters.

"When he was in the eighth grade, he was probably the second-best player on the team behind me," Scott Favre said. "I was a junior at the time."

Once, in an American Legion baseball game, Favre doubled in his first at-bat, homered in his second and came to the plate a third time with the bases loaded. The manager called for an intentional walk.

"They threw three pitches outside," said Mike Ross, the home-plate umpire that day. "Before the fourth pitch, Brett turned to me and said, 'Do you think I'm going to let them walk me?' I said, 'You don't have much choice.'

"They threw the fourth pitch outside and he reached out and hit it for a ground-rule double over the right-field fence."

(top) Baby Brett (above) Favre with his dad

In football, Brett was big and strong and loved the physical part of the game. He might have made an outstanding high school linebacker or safety but rarely got the chance to show what he could do on that side of the ball.

That's because all three Favre boys were quarterbacks at Hancock, not so much because they were indispensable athletes (though that was largely true) but because Irvin

knew he could depend on them to show up for practice.

"Back then, there were days you'd have 18 or 20 kids to practice with," Gaudin said. "If one of them missing is your quarterback, you can't hardly do much. So Scott was a quarterback when he came through and it was obvious Brett was going to be a quarterback.

"Irvin got flak about that. People said, 'He's the head coach. He's just making his kids the quarterbacks.' He'd talk to me about it and say, 'You know, the reason I do this is because I know they're going to be at practice. They ain't got no choice.' There was a lot of logic to that."

Big Irv, as he was known, was a good athlete himself, a former star baseball player at the University of Southern Mississippi. As a coach, he was no-nonsense, a man whose authority was unquestioned. He told Bonita, in no uncertain terms, that if one of their sons was ever hurt, she'd better not run down on his gull-dang football field.

"I always thought he was straight out of the Marines," said Stevie Haas, who owns the Broke Spoke bar in Kiln and knew the Favres because Haas' parents owned a grocery store. "He reminded me of a drill sergeant. He had that deep voice and wore a flat-top (hair cut)."

Haas went out for football at Hancock. He lasted just one day.

"It was 95 degrees and we ran and ran and ran," he said. "I asked Irv if we were going to run less the next day. He said, 'We'll probably run more.' That was all I needed to hear.

"I didn't show up for practice the next day and he came looking for me in my parents' store. I was stocking shelves and he came back there yelling, 'Candy! Where's Candy?'"

Said Jeff Favre: "Dad was hard on everybody. Old school. He'd run a lot of people off the team. He didn't put up with much (expletive), that's for sure."

Big Irv's toughness was legendary and undoubtedly rubbed off on his impressionable sons.

"Irv was up on the roof one day doing some stuff at the house," said Clark Henegan, one of Brett's best friends. "He fell off the roof and landed on his head on the concrete. He got up, dazed, blood running down his face, and wouldn't go to the hospital. I saw it happen myself.

"They'd start crying because he threw so hard and, I mean, he may hit you."

Bonita Favre,
Brett's mom, recalling his days as a Little League pitcher

"Brett thinks when you get hurt, put some ice on it, you'll be all right. That was Irv's patented move right there. Broken leg? Put some ice on it, you'll be all right. Get back out there."

In the early 1970s, just after he took over the football program at Hancock North Central, Big Irv attended a coaching clinic conducted by Alabama legend Paul "Bear" Bryant. He came back to Hancock and installed Bryant's version of the wishbone offense.

Like the Bear, Big Irv did not believe in throwing the football unless it was absolutely necessary. Though his sons had exceptional arms, he wasn't going to change his offense just to accommodate them.

"People always say, 'Man, y'all could throw. Why didn't you throw the ball?'" Scott Favre said. "Dad wasn't going to do it. He believed in his offense and he wasn't going to showcase his sons."

Brett, in fact, rarely attempted more than five passes in a high school game. After Irv begged his alma mater to take a look at his son, Southern Miss dispatched offensive line coach Mark McHale, who sat in the stands as Brett led his team to victory but threw only a handful of passes.

When McHale told Irv he couldn't recommend that Southern Miss sign Brett as a quarterback based on what he had seen, Irv asked him to come back the next week, promising to open up the offense.

"So McHale went the next week, and Brett threw it six or seven times," said Regiel Napier, the former sports information director at Southern Miss. "To Irv, that was airing it out."

Once, during Brett's senior year, Scott returned from college to watch a game and was standing on the sideline. Hancock North Central was ahead by two or three touchdowns, and Scott told Brett he was going to try to talk their father into letting him throw the ball.

photos courtesy of WTMJ-TV

(above) Favre scores a touchdown for Hancock North Central High School.

"I eased over to Dad: 'Hey, Dad, why don't you let Brett throw it a little bit?'" Scott said with a chuckle. "He turned and looked at me and said, 'Who's coaching this damned team? Get your ass up in the stands with your mom.' I looked over at Brett and said, 'I think you're on your own, buddy.'"

When Brett did get a chance to show off his arm – mostly in pick-up games at home or on the baseball diamond – he left onlookers shaking their heads in amazement.

While pitching in a Little League game once, he hit a batter in the helmet with a blazing fastball, knocking the boy down. The next batter got halfway to home plate, dropped his bat and started sobbing.

"There were kids who wouldn't bat against him," said Bonita Favre. "They'd start crying because he threw so hard and, I mean, he may hit you."

Later, as the starting third baseman as an eighth-grader at Hancock North Central, Brett cleanly fielded a sharp grounder and proceeded to overthrow the first baseman by five feet. The ball sailed over the dugout, flew through an open window on the opposing team's bus and pin-balled around the interior.

"I looked at Brett and said, 'What the hell was that?'" said Scott, who was pitching. "He said, 'Hell, I caught the ball.' I said, 'Yeah, but you think maybe you could get the throw to first base?' He said, 'I'm working on that.'"

Though Brett rarely got the chance to show off his arm during football games, there was no question he was blessed with one-in-a-billion talent.

One of his elementary school teachers, Billy Ray Dedeaux, recalled Brett throwing 50-yard passes in the fifth grade.

"He could chuck it," Dedeaux said. "The kids who caught the ball from him said it was like a bullet."

Favre sat out his sophomore football season with mononucleosis. He begged Bonita to take him to the doctor every Friday for blood screenings; every Friday the doctor told him he wasn't ready to play. (To this day, Bonita said, Brett refuses to drink out of another person's glass, believing he caught mono by sharing water bottles at football practice.)

That fall, Brett took out his frustration by throwing passes to the junior varsity players.

Chad Favre, a cousin, recalled being on the receiving end of those passes, which usually resulted in two rows of tiny bruises on his chest – marks left by the eyelets of the shoulder pad laces.

"Me and a couple of other guys were playing with one of those little junior varsity footballs once," Chad said. "Brett came out and said, 'Go deep, go deep.' I'm

Favre with future wife Deanna Tynes.

running, I'm running, I'm running. He was in one end zone and when I finally caught the ball and staggered a couple steps, I was in the other end zone. So he threw that ball about 90 yards. He just had a cannon."

An unwavering confidence in his arm strength enabled Favre to make throws few other quarterbacks would even attempt. It also got him into trouble on occasion, when he forced the ball into coverage.

"When we used to play, somebody might break loose 50 yards down there, wide open, and somebody else might come across the middle with a guy all over him," Peterson said. "Where do you think Brett is going to throw? He's going to throw to that guy who's got 16 inches between him (and the defender)."

But a strong arm and a stubborn streak will not get you 253 consecutive starts in the NFL. Favre displayed other traits as a youth that would serve him well throughout his career.

First and foremost: his ultra-competitiveness.

"He's always been that way," Peterson said. "It don't matter if he's playing ping-pong or throwing marbles. He wants to win."

Once, Favre talked Peterson into entering a Punt, Pass & Kick contest with him. When Peterson won a trophy, Favre could barely contain his anger.

"He was so mad," Peterson said. "He was fired up."

After the high school football season ended, Gaudin supervised once-a-week touch football games in the winter. He picked one team, Favre picked another, and they'd go at it.

"You'd have thought we were playing for the Super Bowl," Gaudin said. "It was just touch football but we were getting after it. Drizzling, rain, cold, it didn't matter.

HANCOCK BANK

MEMBER FDIC

Handy 24

COKER POINT VIDEO

SELF SERVE

UNL. 1.21
UNL. PLUS 1.27
SUPER UNL. 1.39

WELCOME TO BRETT FAVRE COUNTRY

Jolly Rogers PRINTING
COPIES · FAX · UPS
OPEN MONDAY - FRIDAY 8 A.M. - 4 P.M.

GO PACKERS!
WAY BRETT
BAY

Welc to
Kiln,
Hom
Brett

Me and Brett would get in arguments if my team beat his or his beat mine.

"That was the No. 1 thing: his competitiveness."

Favre also was dedicated in the off-season. During a time when high school athletes rarely trained for a sport year-round, he lifted weights three or four days a week. Friends remember him throwing the ball alone, over and over, or enlisting Deanna Tynes, then his girlfriend and now his wife, to catch passes.

"Brett would throw the ball so hard, Irvin would come out and fuss at him," Bonita Favre said. "Deanna wouldn't let on. She was going to catch 'em."

Years later, Bonita could scarcely believe what her son achieved on the football field. She attended a Packers pre-season game in August 2005 and shared a luxury box with the mother of a soldier who had been killed in Iraq.

The subject turned to heroes.

"The mother said, 'They call your son a hero, and my son is a hero,'" Bonita said. "I said, 'I know, but I just can't see it that way.' She said, 'I looked it up in the dictionary and a hero is an ordinary person doing an extraordinary job.' So I guess that's true."

Favre would return regularly to his hometown, never putting on airs or bragging about his exploits in the NFL. He still enjoyed throwing the ball around with his brothers and a few years ago took great delight in spraining one of Peterson's fingers with a bullet pass.

Haas, wiping down the bar at the Broke Spoke just days before Hurricane Katrina smashed through Hancock County, paused to reflect on the local legend.

"Brett ain't changed none," Haas said. "He seems like the same what I can remember from high school. He was just Brett then and he's just Brett now." ❹

Cindy Schutte takes a picture of her husband, Russ Schutte, and son Sam, 12, and daughter Katrina, 14, in front of a sign in Kiln, Miss., honoring Favre. "We drove 400 miles out of our way to see this," said Russ Schutte. The Monroe, Wis., family was driving to Florida in 1997 for a vacation and didn't want to miss the opportunity.

LIFE OF THE PARTY

Favre caught on quickly in college

By Gary D'Amato

Hattiesburg, Miss. – On the evening of Sept. 18, 1987, Brett Favre and Chris Ryals holed up in their room in the football dormitory at the University of Southern Mississippi for a long night of introspection.

Neither freshman had played in the Golden Eagles' season-opener two weeks earlier, a 38-6 thumping at Alabama. Both expected to be redshirted.

It was time for some serious goal-setting.

"We sat there and just got drunk, drunk, drunk," Ryals said. "We figured if we drank eight beers, then seven, then six. . . we figured 36 would make the perfect pyramid. We drank a case and a half.

"That was in the good old days of Johnny Carson and David Letterman. We sat there like two old men, watching TV and drinking beer. Oh, it was beautiful. We completed the pyramid about 2:15 in the morning."

The next afternoon, Southern Miss played host to Tulane at M.M. Roberts Stadium. Early in the game, the Golden Eagles were struggling on offense again and Favre was struggling to stay upright.

"When we ran on the field, he went over to the wall and bent over and ralphed," Ryals said. "Just vomits his guts up right there. He looks like he's about to drop warming up. He's sweating bullets, white as a sheet."

In the third quarter, coach Jim Carmody, frustrated by his offense's ineptitude, did the heretofore unthinkable:

He called the press box and told offensive coordinator Jack White he was putting Favre – a 17 year old freshman – into the game at quarterback.

"Jack said, 'What? I thought we were redshirting him,'" Carmody said with a chuckle.

It was an auspicious debut for the man who would one day lead the Green Bay Packers to victory in Super Bowl XXXI and become one of the National Football League's biggest stars.

That steamy afternoon at "The Rock," Favre trotted unsteadily into a huddle composed mostly of upperclassmen.

"All five offensive linemen were fifth-year seniors and now you've got this young idiot quarterback," Ryals said. "He was hung over. Sick. They all knew he got drunk the night before."

Chris McGee, then a senior wide receiver and team co-captain, at first was puzzled by the crowd's reaction to Favre, who had played high school football some 50 miles south at Hancock North Central.

"Brett came on the field and the stands went wild," McGee said. "I hear the crowd yelling and screaming and I'm trying to figure out what in the hell is going on. I thought somebody in the stands got to fighting or something.

Favre's four-year run as quarterback for the Southern Mississippi Golden Eagles produced a 29-17 record.

"The next thing we know, uncharacteristic of our head coach, we start throwing the football all over the field."

Favre coolly led the Golden Eagles to a come-from-behind, 31-24 victory, throwing two touchdown passes, including the game-winner to McGee.

It was the beginning of the Brett Favre Era at Southern Miss, a memorable four-year run that produced a 29-17 record, and upset victories over Auburn, Alabama and Florida State and two bowl bids.

Favre still holds several school passing records, including career touchdown passes (52), completions (613), attempts (1,169), yards passing (7,695) and total offense (7,606 yards).

And it was in Hattiesburg where Favre's legendary toughness would first become evident.

On July 14, 1990, before the start of training camp for his senior season, Favre suffered serious internal injuries in a car wreck; doctors eventually had to remove 30 inches of his small intestine.

Three weeks after the operation – and 35 pounds lighter – he led Southern Miss to a 27-24 upset over Alabama in Birmingham.

"As far as toughness and leadership and grit and passion for the game, Brett was as good as they come," Carmody said. "The guy loved to play."

That he even got the chance is a story in itself.

Favre was the last recruit Southern Miss signed in 1987 – and then only because another quarterback reneged on his oral commitment. Carmody agreed to take him partly as a favor to Irvin Favre, Brett's father and the coach at Hancock North Central High School who had himself played baseball at Southern Miss.

Mark McHale, the Golden Eagles' offensive line coach, had scouted Favre, but Hancock North Central ran an option offense and Favre had never thrown more than a handful of passes in any game.

"I said, 'How does he throw?'" Carmody said. "Mark said, 'Coach, they hardly throw the ball.' I said, 'Is he a college quarterback?' He said, 'If he's not, he's a big kid and he can maybe play safety.'"

So Favre showed up on campus as a safety / quarterback. In two-a-days, he worked with the offense in the morning

courtesy of WTMJ-TV

Favre as a Southern Mississippi Golden Eagle with E.L. "Doc" Harrington, longtime head athletic trainer at the school.

and the defense in the afternoon.

It wasn't long, however, before Favre got everyone's attention with his arm strength and the incredible velocity on his passes.

"The first morning, I was standing with my back to his group," Carmody said. "I heard this noise, a whooshing sound. I turned around and said, 'What in the world is that?' I coached a long time and I never heard a ball sound like that."

McGee had no idea who Favre was those first few days of training camp, but he was about to find out.

"I ran a little crossing route about 5 yards over the center and sat down and he threw a 100 mph fastball," McGee said. "I caught the ball and threw it back at him and hit him in the helmet with it. I said, 'Look, calm down. I'm only 5 yards from you. You don't have to throw it so hard.'

"We had a little bond from that moment on."

Even before the Tulane game, Carmody had a hunch Favre would be playing and added some drop-back passes to his veer option offense. Favre went 6-4 as a starter, completing 79 of 194 passes for 1,264 yards, with 15 touchdowns and 13 interceptions.

Not that there weren't some growing pains along the way.

On Oct. 10, Favre's 18th birthday, No. 4 Florida State

"Coach, I swear to god, it was whistling."
Alfred Williams,
Southern Mississippi receiver, after catching a pass from Favre

pummeled Southern Miss, 61-10, in Hattiesburg.

"They just beat us – and him – like a drum," Ryals said. "They were singing 'Happy Birthday' to him every time they sacked him. Yeah, he got thrown to the wolves a couple times."

But even the older players on the team admired the way Favre handled himself. He was cool and calm under pressure, a fun-loving cut-up off the field and a cut-throat competitor on it. He had a commanding presence in the huddle and the others instinctively looked up to him.

"Most of the guys on that offense had been around," said John Fox, the radio voice of the Golden Eagles for 27 years. "Brett was 17 years old and looked like he was 13. He'd tell them, 'Shut up. I'm in charge now.' "

Curley Hallman replaced Carmody as head coach before Favre's sophomore season and brought in Jeff Bower to be the offensive coordinator. Under Hallman and Bower, a former QB at Southern Miss, Favre flourished in a pro-style offense.

Bower used timing drills to help Favre develop touch. The quarterback worked on anticipating wide receivers' breaks and throwing to spots, instead of relying on his arm strength to deliver the ball after the receiver got open.

"At the same time, when you've got an arm that big, you think you can get it in a crack at 40 yards and a lot of times he did," Bower said. "His sophomore year, against East Carolina, he made a throw to Alfred Williams and Alfred said he could hear the ball whistling as he was coming out of his break.

"I've never coached anybody who could make the particular throw he made. It was a deep seam and he just drilled it in there. Alfred said, 'Coach, I swear to god, it was whistling.' "

Southern Miss opened the 1989 season, Favre's junior year, at Florida State. The Seminoles had beaten the Golden Eagles the previous two years by the combined score of 90-23.

In the closing minutes, the Golden Eagles trailed, 26-24, but Favre drove the team the length of the field. Hallman

called for a couple running plays to make Florida State use timeouts. On third and goal at the 4, Bower persuaded Hallman to run a play-action pass.

"It was wide open for a score because they had everybody in the box," Bower said. "I had to convince Curley to call it. I said, 'Curley, do you want a touchdown or a field goal?'

"He finally let me call it, so I got Brett on the phone and said, 'Here's the play. He's going to be wide open. It's a score. But the worst thing that can ever happen is if you throw (an interception) or take a sack.' Well, we had two guys wide open and he threw a little balloon out there for a touchdown.

"But I wouldn't have done it with any other quarterback but him."

Before Favre's senior season, Southern Mississippi sports information director Regiel Napier organized a "Favre 4 Heisman" campaign. Realistically, a quarterback from Southern Miss probably wasn't going to win the Heisman Trophy, but Favre at least was a candidate.

"Then he goes out and gets hurt," Napier said. "It was no fun at the time."

Favre was returning home from a day on Ship Island off Biloxi. He was driving his 1989 Nissan Maxima; his brother Scott and friend Keith Loescher were behind him in Scott's pickup.

About a quarter-mile from home, Favre rounded a curve and encountered an oncoming car with its bright lights on. He steered slightly to the right and the tires on the Maxima dipped into loose gravel. He overcorrected with the steering wheel and his car shot across the road, slammed into an embankment and then flew end-over-end, thumping into a pine tree.

"Brett was out cold," Scott Favre said. "I busted the window out with a golf club. We drug him out and left him until the ambulance got there."

Favre suffered significant internal injuries caused by the seat belt restraint and doctors had to remove a portion of his intestines. He sat out the season-opener, a 12-0 victory over Delta State, but was back in the lineup for the upset victory over Alabama the next week.

"There was talk about redshirting him," Fox said. "You know Brett. He said, 'B.S. That ain't happening. I'm playing.' "

Favre started every game the rest of the season. ❹

TRADING PLACES

Wolf hits the jackpot in deal for Favre

By Tom Silverstein

It wasn't just fate or circumstance that brought Brett Favre to Green Bay. It was much, much more.

The trade that swung open the doors of greatness for the future Hall of Fame quarterback was spun out of lessons remembered, memories forgotten and pure, unwavering conviction.

On Feb. 10, 1992, Green Bay general manager Ron Wolf, on his 75th day on the job, traded a first-round draft choice to the Atlanta Falcons for the quarterback who would return the Packers' franchise to the glory of its past. It was the culmination of two years work in which Wolf first identified Favre as the next great NFL quarterback and then pursued him like an animal tracking prey.

Now that people can speak of Favre's career in the past, and all that is left are the memories of his cannon arm and brazen toughness, they should recognize the trade that Wolf made as one of the greatest of all time.

"I feel very ecstatic what he accomplished," Wolf said. "...He's worth a lot more than a first-round draft choice. I really don't care how they recognize it, but I have to use that Bum Phillips line: I don't know if it's the best, but it won't take long to call the roll."

It was fate and circumstance that Wolf and Favre weren't paired together much earlier.

The story has been written often about how Wolf, then an assistant to New York Jets general manager Dick Steinberg, had Favre ranked as the No. 1 player in the 1991 draft and tried desperately to move into the first round to select him (the Jets didn't have a first-round pick).

But it was a lesson Wolf had learned 21 years earlier that first put him onto Favre.

As a young scout with the Oakland Raiders, Wolf had traveled through the back roads of Arkansas in dangerous, stormy weather to see a promising, young linebacker named Bill Bergey. By the time he got there, he was exhausted and the report he wrote was incoherent.

Wolf never returned to make another evaluation and was stung when Bergey went on to become rookie of the year and a four-time Pro Bowl selection for the Philadelphia Eagles. He vowed never to make the same mistake.

So when, in 1990, Southern Mississippi assistant coach Thamas Coleman begged him to come back and take a second look at a young quarterback named Favre, Wolf, remembering the mistake he made with Bergey, did. He put on tape of Favre's junior season and saw a different player from the one who had been affected his senior year by a car accident that resulted in 30 inches of his intestines being removed.

Though Wolf had to sit back and watch his close friend and former Raiders associate Ken Herock steal Favre with the 33rd selection in the draft, one spot ahead of the Jets, he never lost hope that one day Favre would be his. For the next year, Wolf kept close tabs on Favre, and when he was hired to be the Packers' general manager on Nov. 27,

Favre was drafted in the second round by the Atlanta Falcons in 1991, but coach Jerry Glanville wanted nothing to do with him and he played in only two games. The Falcons traded him to the Packers in February 1992 for a first-round draft choice.

Falcons coach Jerry Glanville said during a 1991 exhibition game that it would take a plane crash for him to put Favre in.

1991, he made obtaining Favre a priority.

In Atlanta, Favre had become a whipping boy for flamboyant coach Jerry Glanville, who never approved of Herock's decision to draft him and once said during an exhibition game that it would take a plane crash for him to put Favre into the game. The more Glanville ignored the wild and unbridled Favre, the more Favre rebelled.

According to an Atlanta Journal-Constitution story, Glanville had four rules: 1) Be on time. 2) Prepare all week to play. 3) Spill your guts on the field. 4) Only accept victory.

"If he'd have got to 3 and 4, he'd have been fine," Glanville once told the paper. "But you had to get past 1 and 2."

Favre's behavior was immature and unprofessional. He stayed out late, he showed up late and fell asleep in meetings. As he once said, "I'm sure I didn't help my cause by trying to drink up Atlanta."

Herock doesn't know why Favre acted the way he did.

"He had a big ego," Herock said. "His comments to me in the locker room were, 'They need to play me. I'm better than those guys.' We had a Pro Bowl quarterback (Chris Miller) and I could see why he was still sitting, but he felt he was better than them. Why he was doing what he was doing, I have no idea. I think if you ask him he probably couldn't answer it either."

Favre's behavior put Herock in a tough spot.

Glanville thought so little of Favre that he refused to make him Miller's backup and Herock was forced to trade for Billy Joe Tolliver. Days after Herock made the trade, he went on the road, thinking Favre was still the No. 2, but when he came back, Glanville already had made Tolliver the top backup.

Wolf, meanwhile, was keenly aware of what was going on in Atlanta. During the summer of Favre's rookie season, he traveled to Portland to scout a scrimmage between the Falcons and Seattle Seahawks. Favre lit up the place.

BRETT FARVE

Even a future Hall of Famer can get his name misspelled on his rookie card.

"He was the star of that game," Wolf said. "At that scrimmage, he did everything. He substantiated everything I believed in that he was capable of doing and he did it."

Talk about fate. It was the only time Favre ever did anything in Atlanta. Several days later in an exhibition game against the Los Angeles Rams, Favre was terrible. He looked like someone who didn't belong in the NFL.

"He looked pathetic," Herock said. "He's throwing interceptions and he looks like he's never played the game. He had a long ways to go."

As Favre's season deteriorated, leaving him to hold the clipboard and run the scout team, Herock came under increasing pressure to make good on the pick he made. Herock had overruled Glanville in the draft room to take Favre over Browning Nagle, and now it was clear Glanville and his offensive coordinator, June Jones, wanted nothing to do with Favre.

On Dec. 1, 1991, the Packers played at Atlanta. Herock came up to Wolf in the press box and said, "If you want to see Favre throw you have to look at him now because they won't let him throw during pregame warm-ups." Legend has it that Wolf rushed down to the field and liked what he saw so much that it convinced him to make the deal.

The truth is that Wolf never made it to the field to see Favre. Cameras and reporters were following him around and he couldn't break away in time to see Favre throw. His decision to trade for Favre had been made during that scrimmage in Portland. Herock's offering to come down and see Favre throw in warm-ups told him that a deal was possible.

"What that told me was that I now had a chance to get Brett Favre as a player," Wolf said. "Why else would he tell me that?

"From that point on, I spent four or five days a week talking to Ken Herock trying to somehow massage it and get this so first of all we don't lose him and secondly this can be an eventuality. They wanted to get rid of him and I just didn't want that thing to get cold."

Wolf said he intended all along to give up the second of two first-round draft choices the Packers had in 1992. He never let Herock know that, however, and continually told him he would not give up anything more than a second-round pick.

"I was going to give them a first," Wolf said. "Obviously, I didn't start at a first, but I was going to give them a first. I had made my mind up and it had already been approved so we were going to go with that regardless."

Herock was really struggling with having to trade Favre. He didn't want to do it. He brought in Glanville and Jones to meet with Taylor Smith, who was running the Falcons' operation for his father and the team's owner, Rankin Smith. He told Taylor Smith what he thought of Favre and then had Glanville and Jones express their thoughts.

Then he said he would try to get a first-round pick for Favre. All along, he figured he never would get it and he went into negotiations asking for more than that in the hopes no one would bite and he could come back to Smith and tell him no one was interested.

Herock grew up in the Pittsburgh area and his lasting childhood memory was the Pittsburgh Steelers cutting Johnny Unitas. He could never understand how a team could get rid of a guy who would become the greatest quarterback in NFL history, and over the years he had always held onto players longer than he probably should because of that memory.

But for some reason, the memory faded when it came to the Favre deal.

"Maybe I lost sight of the thing," Herock said. "Everyone was telling me how bad he was. That's all I kept hearing. And there was a possibility we could recover a first for a guy we drafted with a second. There was nothing there that said, 'Ken, you're right and they're wrong.' Everything was working against me."

Wolf continued to put pressure on Herock and finally in February the two got serious.

"It happened real quickly. We were sitting there hammering, hammering, hammering and I kept saying, 'I'm not going any higher than a two,'" Wolf said. "I needed them to say something to me and they said the words: 'We can't let him go unless we get a one.'

"'Well, are you saying we have a deal if I give you a one?'" Wolf said.

The answer was yes and the deal was made.

The rest, as they say, is history.

"When I got there, this was the worst team in professional football," Wolf said. "When I left it had the second-best won-lost record in the NFL, and two years later it had the best won-lost record in the NFL and still does since 1992 when Brett Favre took over.

"That's his accomplishment and no one thought that would happen in Green Bay, Wisconsin. And that's my sense of pride right there." ❹

A SUPERSTAR IS BORN

Favre bursts onto the NFL scene in 1992

By Bob McGinn

The question came out of left field, in one of Brett Favre's first sit-down interviews as a Green Bay Packer, three days after he repeatedly ran all over the place seemingly without rhyme or reason in the intrasquad scrimmage before 22,000 fans at Lambeau Field.

It was Aug. 5, 1992. At that point, Favre was coming off a lousy rookie season in Atlanta and had done nothing to demonstrate he was any better than the Packers' Don Majkowski, Mike Tomczak or Ty Detmer.

The 22-year-old Favre sat in reflection as the names of some of the great quarterbacks in the National Football League – Dan Marino, John Elway, Troy Aikman and Jeff George – were cited for his consideration.

Surely, he was asked, you lack the pure physical talent needed to be included with that crowd, don't you?

"I can be," Favre said, and when his startled interviewer looked up, Favre didn't change his impassive expression. "I can do anything they can do. There's nobody in the league that I look at in awe. I just haven't proven it yet."

Less than five months later, Favre would be voted to the NFC Pro Bowl team alongside Steve Young and Aikman.

Ten years later, newly renovated Lambeau Field would start being sold out for that same intrasquad scrimmage.

And Favre deserves substantial credit for everything connected to the Packers' phenomenon.

"He certainly is to the Packers what I'm sure Joe Montana was to the San Francisco 49ers early in both of their careers," general manager Ron Wolf said in spring 1993. "He's obviously our building block."

Even before training camp opened, Favre endeared himself to some of his most important teammates. One night in April, Favre went out for Mexican food and then a few beers at McSwiggan's, a tavern on Green Bay's east side.

"Some guy was there for a bachelor party with a bunch of people and he was pretty inebriated and got in my face," former Packers guard Rich Moran said. "Next thing you know, Brett flew over my shoulder, grabbed the guy and pinned him against the wall. It was unbelievable because I really didn't even know Brett yet. It was a conversation piece in the locker room. By the time the season started, Brett was our guy."

Other than displaying a cannon arm, Favre had a rough summer. Balls were sailing all over the practice field just as they did in exhibition games, when he tossed six interceptions compared with one touchdown pass. His passer rating was 46.0.

In the game that started his Green Bay legend, Favre celebrates after throwing the winning touchdown pass against Cincinnati on Sept. 20, 1992. Favre had entered the game after Don Majkowski injured his left ankle on a sack by the Bengals' Tim Krumrie – a native of Eau Claire, Wis., who attended Mondovi (Wis.) High School and played for the University of Wisconsin. Favre began his record streak as a starter the following week.

AN ERA BEGINS

Below is the official NFL play-by-play that shows Brett Favre entering the Packers' game against Cincinnati in Week 3 of the 1992 season after starter Don Majkowski injured his ankle. From then on, Favre would never relinquish the job. His record streak of 253 starts at quarterback began the following week against Pittsburgh. Favre had played the second half of the game in Week 2 against Tampa Bay, but Majkowski resumed his role as starter against the Bengals.

Favre fumbled four times in the game, but won it for the Packers, 24-23, on a 35-yard TD pass to Kitrick Taylor with 13 seconds remaining.

```
                    Cincinnati Bengals vs Green Bay Packers at Lambeau Field
   NFL Play By Play                1st Quarter                 09/20/92   Page 1
```

Green Bay Packers at 9:10
1-10-GB36   V.Workman right guard to GB39 for 3 yards (T...
2-7-GB39   D.Majkowski pass incomplete to B.McGee.
3-7-GB39   **D.Majkowski sacked at GB31 for -8 (T.Krumrie). #7 QB left ankle twisted.**
4-15-GB31   P.McJulien punts 40 to CB29, Center-F.Winters. C.Pickens ret. to CB34 for 5 (R.Mitchell; B.Dent).

Cincinnati Bengals at 8:05
1-10-CB34   H.Green right end to CB35 for 1 yard (J.Holland, T.Bennett).
2-9-CB35   B.Esiason pass is INTERCEPTED by J.Holland at CB47. (J.Holland).
            J.Holland to CB45 for 2 return yards. J.Holland FUMBLES, and recovers at CB45.

Green Bay Packers at 7:29
1-10-CB45   **B.Favre pass to S.Sharpe, pushed out of bounds at CB39 for 6 yards (E.Thomas).**
2-4-CB39   V.Workman up middle to CB36 for 3 yards (F.Vinson).
3-1-CB36   B.Favre up middle to CB35 for 1 yard (L.Rogers; T.Krumrie).   R1
1-10-CB35   V.Workman left tackle, pushed out of bounds at CB26 for 9 yards (B.Bussey; E.Thomas).
2-1-CB26   V.Workman right guard to CB19 for 7 yards (T.Krumrie; A.Mitz).   R2
1-10-CB19   V.Workman up middle to CB17 for 2 yards (J.F... Krumrie).
2-8-CB17   V.Workman l...ble to CB19 (T.Kr...   ...Kru...touched at CB19 for

(opposite) Favre gets up in front of coach Mike Holmgren and QB Don Majkowski after scrambling for yardage in the second half against the Tampa Bay Buccaneers on Sept. 13, 1992, in Tampa. Holmgren had benched Majkowski after the first half of the 31-3 loss. Third-string quarterback Ty Detmer (in cap) stands next to Majkowski.

"The guy who got the most attention was so down to earth and so humble. You did not want to get that guy hit."

Rich Moran,
Packers guard in 1992

After an overtime loss to Minnesota, the Packers were being annihilated by the lowly Tampa Bay Buccaneers in Tampa when coach Mike Holmgren benched Majkowski at halftime and stuck in Favre.

Months later, Favre mustered the courage to review his play in Tampa and said, "I kind of cringed."

On his first regular-season play, Favre rolled to his right and fired a point-blank-range bullet toward fullback Harry Sydney. Defensive end Ray Seals batted it back into Favre's face, giving Favre the dubious distinction of being the recipient of his first aerial. The play went for minus-7 yards.

Amazingly enough, that possession lasted 9 minutes and 23 seconds, thanks mainly to two Tampa Bay penalties on third downs. Chris Jacke capped Favre's first drive with a field goal, but his three other possessions went nowhere in the 31-3 debacle.

Back at Lambeau Field in Week 3, Majkowski went down with ligament damage in his left ankle on the Packers' sixth play when he held the ball too long and was sacked by Cincinnati nose tackle Tim Krumrie. "Majik" wouldn't be healthy enough even to hold until four weeks later.

What will never be forgotten is Favre's thunderbolt in the final 13 seconds, a touchdown pass of 35 yards to Kitrick Taylor in the right corner of the end zone that made Green Bay a 24-23 winner.

What few recall about Brett Lorenzo Favre's rite of passage that sunny, 70-degree afternoon is how it started out. He was at fault on all four of his fumbles, blew multiple blitz reads and put the team into some bizarre formations that left Holmgren a frazzled wreck.

"I was wondering if they were going to run me out of town," Favre said later. "I told James Campen on the sidelines, 'It's good I'm getting hit like I am because it brings

The 1992 season was Favre's coming-out party, where fans began to see their quarterback's intensely competitive but joyful nature.

you to your senses.' I was shaking. I felt like I took a laxative. Thank God I held it till afterward."

Starting from the 8-yard line and down 23-17 with 1:07 left, the situation was bleaker than bleak. But on the second play, the kid gunned a 42-yard bullet to Sterling Sharpe in front of the Bengals' bench. Three plays later, he unleashed a strike to Taylor on the same route against the same Cover 2 defense just as Taylor crossed the goal line.

Favre ripped off his helmet, brandished it above his head and broke into a madcap tear in the middle of the field. Holmgren got his attention long enough to point out he still had to hold for Jacke's deciding placement.

Game day at Lambeau Field, essentially a home for losers since 1967, was never the same again.

"When all those around you have doubt, he doesn't have the doubt," Wolf said that day. "That's what he possesses."

Favre made his first start the next week against a Pittsburgh team that went 11-5 and looked like a different player in a 17-3 victory. His passer rating of 144.6 showed a maturity that no one thought possible.

The Packers, predicted to finish 4-12 by Pro Football Weekly, lost three in a row, but Favre wasn't playing poorly at all. Holmgren waited until after Favre's third start to anoint him as No. 1.

"But it can always change," said Favre, echoing a fear of failure that stayed with him throughout his career. "You've always got to be on your toes."

Favre's first appearance at the Pontiac Silverdome came on Nov. 1 with the club 2-5 and established as a 10-point underdog. The Packers won, 27-13, as Favre demonstrated qualities that would burn brightly for years to come.

Late in the third quarter, Favre was absolutely crushed by defensive end Robert Porcher and suffered what appeared to be a catastrophic ankle injury. Favre's initial thought was that his career might be over just as Joe Theismann's had been ended by a compound leg fracture on a hit by Lawrence Taylor in 1985.

Well, Favre got up limping but didn't miss a play.

Then, with 4 minutes left, Moran suffered a season-ending knee injury. The first one to Moran's side was Favre, who held his hand until help arrived.

"I was so out of it and had no idea he did that," Moran said. "But you know what? He just made it fun. The guy who got most of the attention was so down to earth and so humble. You did not want to get that guy hit."

Laughing, Moran added: "The other thing that endeared himself to us linemen was his quick release."

Favre was guilty of critical mistakes the next week on the road against the Giants in a 27-7 defeat. Then the Packers put together a six-game winning streak for the first time since 1965.

It started in memorable fashion against Bud Carson's vaunted Philadelphia defense in Milwaukee. Late in the first quarter, Reggie White and Andy Harmon sandwiched Favre, leaving him with a minor separation of the left shoulder. Majkowski threw down his warm-up jacket, but Favre wouldn't leave.

At halftime, team physician Clarence Novotny injected Favre with the painkiller xylocaine. The Packers won, 27-24, Favre had a rating of 89.8 and White cited Favre as a salient reason why he signed with Green Bay six months later.

"He's the best young quarterback I've seen," White said after the game.

Favre began his mastery of the Bears in Week 11. He came through in the end to hold off Tampa Bay. And he played in his first snowstorm and was on fire in a demolition of Detroit.

Shaking off a poor start, Favre bounced back late to help upset the talented Houston Oilers in the Astrodome, 16-14. Then he had a rating of 97.7 as the Packers hammered the Los Angeles Rams, 28-13, on an 8-degree Sunday at Lambeau Field.

"I've been a part of broadcasting in this league for a long time," CBS play-by-play man Verne Lundquist said during the telecast of the second Bears game. "If (Favre) becomes a real player in this league, he will also become a huge star. He is one of the most compelling personalities I've ever been around."

During an early October telecast, former Rams coach and CBS analyst John Robinson said: "This kid has got some Bobby Layne in him or some Terry Bradshaw in him. Or maybe a combination of both. He has been a delight to watch."

Suddenly, the Packers were 9-6 and on the brink of the playoffs, but two things needed to happen. First, Washington (9-6) had to lose on Saturday afternoon as an eight-point favorite at home against the Raiders (6-9). Second, the Packers had to win in the Metrodome on

Benny Sieu

Sunday afternoon against the Vikings (10-5), who had won the NFC Central and had nothing at stake.

In dramatic fashion, the Raiders did upset the Redskins, 21-20. So the Packers went into Week 16 with a playoff berth riding on the outcome for the first time since Bart Starr's last game as coach at Soldier Field in 1983.

Reading a blitz perfectly, Favre lobbed a 29-yard completion to Jackie Harris on the first possession and Green Bay led, 7-0. But that was all she wrote. In a game rated a tossup by oddsmakers, the Vikings rolled, 27-7.

On the tape, you see Favre forcing the ball to his only competent wide receiver, Sharpe, and being intercepted three times by the free safety, Vencie Glenn. You see the great pass-rush tandem of John Randle and Chris Doleman all over Favre but the youngster standing firm and taking just one sack. And you see Holmgren alternately mad as hell and understanding of what his first team and his meal ticket had accomplished.

The next July, quarterbacks coach Steve Mariucci would say, "I would rather have nobody else besides Brett Favre as our starting quarterback. To me, he's the exact right guy for the Packers at this point in time."

Tough times were right around the corner, but the cornerstone with a No. 4 jersey draped over it had been laid for the glories to come. ❹

(opposite) Mark Carrier of the Bears tries unsuccessfully to keep Favre from scoring a touchdown during the Packers' 17-3 victory over Chicago at Soldier Field on Nov. 22, 1992. (left) Brett Who? Favre once was unknown enough that, like all new Packers, he needed his name taped on his helmet during practice.

William Meyer

PACKERS ROLL THE DICE

Holmgren banks on his young quarterback

By Lori Nickel

Mike Holmgren paced the field for another training camp practice in August 1993. The most popular question around the National Football League is a personal one:

Is Brett Favre a one-year wonder or the real deal?

Everyone is asking, except Holmgren.

In 1992, Favre went from Green Bay's bench to the Pro Bowl as the youngest quarterback ever to make it to Hawaii. A year later, the Packers have let Don Majkowski go and have brought Reggie White in, but a fact remains.

The Green Bay Packers have been to the playoffs just twice in Favre's young lifetime – in 1972 and 1982. They've not had back-to-back winning seasons since 1967.

Still, when Favre walks into practice during training camp, Packers fans chant "Super Bowl" the second they spot him.

Indeed, in these next two years, everything would change for both the quarterback and the franchise.

Of course, it wouldn't always be easy.

Favre started out the season with eight interceptions against his five touchdowns. Green Bay (1-3) was heading into pivotal games with Denver and Tampa Bay – the Packers held on for a close victory against the Broncos and then went on a tear in Tampa.

But Favre won three games on his own for the team that year.

Against New Orleans, the Packers' defense forced five turnovers and got five sacks. The offense struggled, but in the end, Favre connected on a 54-yard pass to a bloody and bruised Sterling Sharpe, who had to close an eye to make the catch with about 40 seconds left in the game. Four plays later, Chris Jacke's 36-yard field goal led to the Packers' 19-17 victory in the Superdome, a homecoming for Favre, who grew up an hour away. It also kept the Packers' playoff hopes alive.

Two weeks later, Favre had one of those games in Lambeau that defies logic. The numbers weren't great, but the result was a victory. The offense managed 13 points and 259 total yards against a lousy Tampa Bay defense, and Favre completed 23 of 36 passes for 152 yards. It wasn't a banner day for the offense.

But when the Packers needed Favre most, he was at his best.

He led the Packers on a 75-yard scoring drive late. After going for a running touchdown on second and goal, he was hit so hard by Tampa Bay end Shawn Price and safety Barney Bussey that his feet went flying above his head.

Favre had to call a timeout to regroup from the thigh injury. Holmgren summoned backup Ty Detmer, but Favre, struggling just to walk, returned to toss a 2-yard touchdown

Favre emerges from the dugout to take the field for a game at Milwaukee County Stadium in 1993. The Packers played several home games in Milwaukee each year from 1953 through 1994.

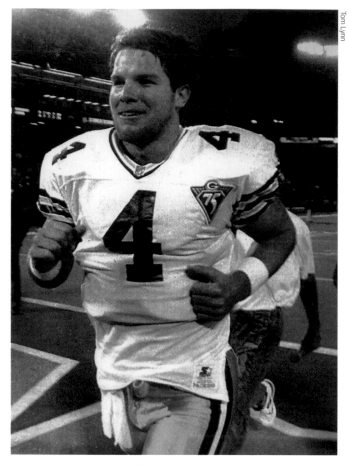

Tom Lynn

> ## *"I want to hug him more than strangle him, but it's close."*
>
> **Mike Holmgren,**
> Packers coach

pass to Sharpe, giving the Packers the 13-10 victory. It was the third straight Green Bay victory and the Packers' third straight, fourth-quarter, come-from-behind triumph.

No one questioned the kid's toughness. He threw a block in an exhibition game that charged up the crowd and his own teammates.

But, for sure, it was that arm that would make him the next Troy Aikman or Steve Young, players whom he joined at the Pro Bowl after the 1992 season. Holmgren knew it was just a matter of work, experience and lots and lots of patience. But there were times the coach looked as if he was going to burst. The crimson would begin in his cheeks, then spread to his neck, his ears, and forehead. The headset didn't always pinch his temples tightly enough to remain there.

On the field, Favre seemed as if he was rolling the dice at one of those casinos back home.

"I want to hug him more than strangle him, but it's close," Holmgren said at the time.

Favre had just four games out of 18 (regular season and playoffs) in which he did not throw an interception. It had to have been tempting to Holmgren to bench Favre. He was young, maybe he needed the lesson. But Holmgren never did. The coach saw what outsiders did not: Favre putting in 12-hour workdays, coming in on Tuesdays, the off day, to lift weights, run and watch film. The son of a coach, Favre did everything he could to get better.

Favre even jotted down ideas in his playbooks and reminders on sticky notes.

So Holmgren gave Favre his unconditional faith and told him they would be attached at the hip, whether that meant great things in the future, or disaster.

"He said that, he really did," Favre recalled in 2005. "And there were times I questioned it, times I questioned how serious he was. He always came through. I know I

(above) Favre runs off the field after a 28-24 playoff victory at Detroit on Jan. 8, 1994. His 40-yard, across-the-field touchdown pass to Sterling Sharpe with 55 seconds left won the game. (opposite) Wide receiver Sterling Sharpe and Favre embrace after they combined on a TD pass against Tampa in 1993. Sharpe was Favre's favorite target before retiring because of injury after the 1994 season.

made that decision more difficult for him. Week in and week out, should I replace him or just give him a break? He always came through.

"That's a good example of sticking with your player through tough times, especially early on. In order for a guy to appreciate the success and the good times, he has

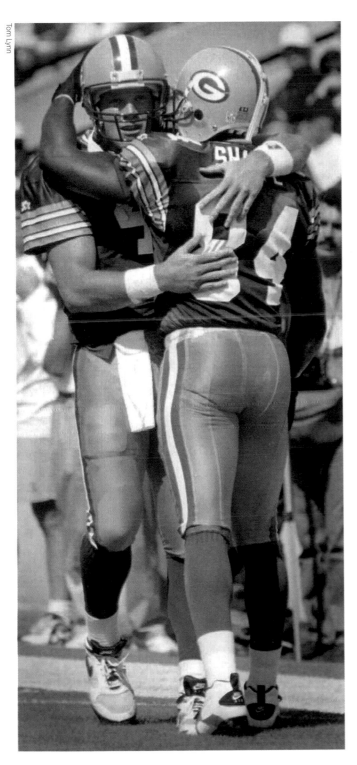

to appreciate the low and the fight that it takes to get through them.

"It makes me appreciate them. I know Mike would probably say, 'I am glad I stuck with him.' He could have easily went a different direction. No one would have ever questioned it at the time, but now look where we are today. I'm so thankful for it. But he did tell me that, probably my second year. My first year. First year, I played well and I think I surprised myself and everyone else. My second year, reality kind of set in, that's when he said, 'Look, I'm going to stick with you one way or another, so, I don't want you to feel like you have to look over your shoulder,' and that did make it easier for me."

In just his second year, Favre already was among the game's elite. His 522 attempts and 318 completions were second to John Elway. His 3,303 passing yards put him second in the NFC. His 19 touchdown passes placed him third.

Even better for Titletown, the Packers were back in the playoffs.

In the season finale, Favre threw four interceptions in a 30-20 loss at Detroit.

Six days later, again at the Silverdome, this time in the NFC wild-card playoff game, Favre jogged left and threw a 40-yard touchdown pass to Sharpe in the right corner of the end zone with 55 seconds left to beat the Lions, 28-24.

After the game, Favre said: "Last week, everyone had written me off – I was terrible, I didn't need to be here – whatever. But I knew my abilities, this team knew my abilities, Mike knew. None of them gave up on me. All last week I knew the people who count care about me. I just wanted to prove to them that I still had it."

Green Bay lost the next week at Dallas, but the Packers clearly had reinvented themselves. A 4-12 team in 1991, they were a dangerous club on the rise two years later.

And it all began with Favre.

At one point very early in his career, Favre was the lowest-paid starting quarterback in the NFL at $360,000 a year.

After the end of the 1993 season, Favre became a restricted free agent. The negotiations between agent James "Bus" Cook and general manager Ron Wolf took awhile, and in that span, fans debated in the newspapers

THE PACKERS EXTEND...
SINCERE THANKS TO OUR
MILWAUKEE FANS FOR THEIR
GREAT LOYALTY AND SUPPORT
OVER THE PAST 62 SEASONS.

TODAY'S TMJ 4

00:15

4TH QUARTER	1	2	3	4	T
ATLANTA	3	6	0	8	17
▸GREEN BAY	14	0	0	0	14

3RD DOWN AND 1 ON THE 9

and on the airwaves whether the team should give Favre the $5 million a year he wanted, and the results seemed to be half and half.

Meanwhile, the Los Angeles Rams made an offer and the New Orleans Saints gave Favre a workout. Favre, Cook and then Saints head coach Jim Mora Sr. had dinner, but even back then, at just 24 years old, Favre couldn't see himself as anyone other than a Packer.

"I want to finish my career in Green Bay," he said that summer.

Making it clear to everyone who would listen that he wanted a deal done before training camp began, because he had no intentions of holding out, Favre got the five-year, $19 million blockbuster deal on July 14.

Interestingly, a few weeks later the Packers' top receiver, Sterling Sharpe, did stage a one-day holdout over the 10-year,

Tom Lynn

$15.5 million contract he signed in 1991 and threatened to sit out the season. Assuming a leadership role from the beginning, Favre decided not to censor his opinion over Sharpe's contract issues.

"Sure, Sterling's the guy I've thrown to the most the last two years," said Favre. "But I can't fold my tent, then walk into the huddle and let the others see that I've given up. In my opinion Sterling's under contract, and he should honor that contract. If they give him more money, what's to stop other guys from wanting to renegotiate? The Packers can't do that. Listen, no one's that good."

Sharpe returned and caught a touchdown pass to kick off the 1994 season with a Green Bay victory against Minnesota.

The Packers were on their way to another 9-7 season.

But even when he played exceptionally, not every game would go Favre's way. Although clearly a smarter and more experienced player in 1994, Favre still did not leave Detroit with a victory on Dec. 4. Though he had his best game of the year with 366 yards passing, the Packers lost, 34-31.

Holmgren told him after the game, "You played a great game, but it wasn't the perfect game."

(opposite and above) In the last Packers game played at County Stadium in Milwaukee, Favre dives into the end zone for the winning touchdown against Atlanta on Dec. 18, 1994.

"That's asking a lot," Favre said.

"It's what we're shooting for. You've got to know that," Holmgren said.

In '93, he threw 24 interceptions and had a quarterback rating of 72.2. In '94, he totaled 3,882 yards, 33 touchdowns and just 14 interceptions that contributed to a 90.7 quarterback rating.

Once again, the Packers would beat Detroit in an NFC wild-card playoff game, only this time at Lambeau. Without Sharpe, who was injured, the Packers generated just one touchdown, on the opening drive in the 16-10 victory.

And once again, the Packers would lose to Dallas and its No. 1 defense, 35-9, in the next round of the playoffs.

Favre was 18 of 35 for 211 yards, no touchdowns and one interception, and he had found an NFC rival for the 1990s.❹

Rick Wood

FAVRE SEIZES FIRST MVP

He outplays several legends in memorable 1995 season

By Tom Silverstein

When he reflects upon the vote that earned him the first of three consecutive Most Valuable Player awards, Brett Favre can't get over the options that were available besides him.

The 1990s were a special era in the National Football League because of the collection of elite athletes that dominated the playing field, many of whom have, and will, find their way into the Hall of Fame.

In 1995, Troy Aikman, Barry Sanders, Emmitt Smith, Deion Sanders, Steve Young, John Elway, Derrick Thomas, Jerry Rice, Dan Marino and Cris Carter were all going strong.

It really wasn't much of a contest though, not after Favre threw for 38 touchdowns – third-most in league history at that time behind Marino's totals of 48 and 44 – and established himself as one of the toughest players in the game with a five-touchdown performance against Chicago a week after suffering sprained ligaments in his ankle.

Favre won the MVP award in a landslide, receiving 69 of 88 votes from a nationwide media panel. Rice, who set an NFL single-season receiving yardage record, was second with 10 votes.

"That first year I won it, I never thought about it," Favre said during the 2005 season. "I'm sure most guys in this locker room consider themselves pretty good, at least to themselves when they go home or whatever. I knew what I was doing was special, but to be the best football player in the world, I don't know if that ever really crossed my mind."

Not even the confident Favre could have predicted '95 would go the way it did. In fact, before the season started there was a lot of concern about the direction the offense would go because Favre had lost his favorite weapon, receiver Sterling Sharpe, to a career-ending neck injury.

Sharpe had so dominated the offense that going into the season, starters-to-be Robert Brooks, Anthony Morgan and Mark Chmura had caught a combined 100 passes the previous season, which represented less than a third of the completions Favre had made that year. There was considerable apprehension about who was going to catch the ball from Favre.

To that end, Packers general manager Ron Wolf swung trades to acquire wide receiver Mark Ingram and tight end Keith Jackson, both of whom balked at coming to Green Bay and reported late, Ingram on Aug. 1 and Jackson Oct. 20. Both wound up making contributions, but when the season was over, it was Brooks and Chmura who had filled the void left by Sharpe's absence.

Head coach Mike Holmgren talks with Favre during a 13-10 loss to Tampa Bay in 1995. Holmgren steered Favre away somewhat from his gunslinger tendencies, but also let the quarterback continue to take chances because of the potential for great rewards.

Tom Lynn

Gary Porter

"I think sometimes you rely too much on one guy, on one phase of the game," said Favre, who from 1992-'94 had completed 983 passes, with 32% going to Sharpe. "You don't know what else is out there. I know you're a little reluctant to throw it there because I had thrown to Sterling in triple coverage and he still caught it.

"But it tells you someone is one-on-one and not covered. If not for Sterling being hurt, who knows what would have happened. But we had to open it up; we had to find someone else, and we did."

Favre had received a taste of what it would be like to play without Sharpe at the end of the '94 season, when his obvious favorite target was hurt in the regular-season finale against Tampa Bay and subsequently ruled out of the playoffs.

That setback forced Favre to look elsewhere in the Packers' two post-season games.

Favre had made tremendous strides in '94, rebounding from an awful '93 season in which he threw 24 interceptions to throw for 3,882 yards and 33 touchdowns with 14 interceptions the next year. It was around then that Packers coach Mike Holmgren finally started showing confidence in Favre's ability to run his offense.

"I think it started at the end of the year," said quarterback Ty Detmer, who was Favre's backup in '95. "That year Brett started off pretty strong and I think Mike started feeling comfortable with Brett and gave him more to handle. That's all Brett needed."

The '95 season started off ominously with a defeat to the Los Angeles Rams, which would turn out to be the Packers' last home loss until Oct. 5, 1998. Favre threw three interceptions and was sacked four times, but much of the offense's troubles were the result of left tackle Ken Ruettgers being sidelined with a back injury.

(opposite) A Dallas Cowboys defender pursues Favre during a 34-24 Packers loss on Oct. 8, 1995, in Texas. The Cowboys later would defeat Green Bay in the playoffs. (left) LeRoy Butler (36) and members of the training staff help Favre off the field after he injured his ankle in a 27-24 loss in Minnesota on Nov. 5, 1995.

Jeffrey Phelps

Benny Sieu

(opposite) Favre is helped after taking a hit during a 24-19 victory over Pittsburgh in 1995 at Lambeau Field. The game cemented Favre's reputation for durability: He had the wind knocked out of him twice, coughed up blood and suffered a concussion. (above) Favre with Steve Mariucci, his quarterback coach in 1995.

Favre bounced back the next week with a big game against the Chicago Bears and gained national attention when, from his own 1-yard line, he pump-faked to Brooks and then threw downfield, completing what wound up being a 99-yard touchdown pass. The Packers won three straight games and five of the next six, with Favre throwing for 14 touchdowns with just three interceptions.

It was at midseason when things took a turn for the worse. Favre played one of his typically awful games at the Pontiac Silverdome (three interceptions) and then was headed for disaster again at the Metrodome in Minneapolis.

Favre had managed to lead the Packers to a touchdown and two field goals in six possessions, when on the team's final drive of the first half, end Derrick Alexander pushed guard Aaron Taylor backward and on top of Favre's legs. Favre, who suffered a severely sprained ankle, went back in the huddle but after a few seconds went down to one knee and then was forced to go to the sideline.

Detmer replaced him and finished out the half. Favre came back to start the second half, but he threw two interceptions, one that helped the Vikings take a 24-16 lead,

and soon Detmer was back in the game. The Packers lost after Detmer was knocked out with torn thumb ligaments and third-stringer T.J. Rubley made the infamous third-and-1 audible that resulted in an interception and cost the Packers a chance to win the game with a field goal. Instead, the Vikings won on Fuad Reviez's field goal with 50 seconds left.

"I felt it pop," Favre said. "I never broke a bone, but I thought something popped, and as soon as you hear something pop, you think it's a bone. I felt the same way with my knee (in '02); I thought I broke my leg. My first thought is this could be awhile. But I seem to heal quicker than a normal guy, and part of it is mental, just pushing yourself."

Favre's badly swollen left ankle turned blue by Monday, and the chances of him playing the next week at home against the Bears appeared minimal. For the next four days, Favre underwent treatment about 20 hours a day, and at the end of the week he took a few snaps in practice to test the ankle.

It wasn't until Sunday, however, when he tested the ankle in pregame warm-ups, that it was determined he would play.

"I've had bruises before, but it turned blue and then it turned yellow," Favre said. "I didn't do anything all week. I think Mike was like, 'I know the son of a (gun) can go out there and tough it out, but how productive will he be?'

"Mike had his mind made up Saturday, but we didn't know until Sunday. Until I went out there and took the first snap, you don't know. I might have just gone, 'I can't do it.' Once the newness wears off and the toughness wears off, 'I just can't do it.' And I was probably as immobile as I've ever been. I couldn't do anything."

Circumstance played right into Favre's hands. The Bears were without their best defensive player, Donnell Woolford, because of injury and then lost another key component, safety Mark Carrier, early in the game. Without two of his best defensive backs, Chicago coach Dave Wannstedt didn't feel confident blitzing Favre and played the first half conservatively.

Favre, with his left foot wrapped up like a postal package, took three- and five-step drops and proceeded to

Tom Lynn

Rick Wood

(opposite) Favre heads to the locker room after leading the Packers to their biggest victory since the Lombardi era, a 27-17 playoff victory over San Francisco on Jan. 6, 1996, at Candlestick Park. (above) Packers fans display their loyalty by greeting the team hours after Dallas defeated Green Bay in the NFC Championship Game in Texas on Jan. 14, 1996. Favre (blue blazer) and backup quarterback Jim McMahon walk past hundreds of fans after arriving at Austin Straubel International Airport in Green Bay.

carve up the Bears' defense. He completed a 17-yard screen pass for a touchdown to Edgar Bennett, then a 29-yard touchdown pass to Brooks and then a 1-yard scoring strike to Dorsey Levens.

At the end of the first half and into the second, Wannstedt started blitzing, but by then Favre had reached a comfort level in the pocket and burned the Bears for big gains, forcing them to back off. When it was all over, Favre had completed 25 of 33 passes for 336 yards and a career-high five touchdowns.

"I thought he was in a zone," quarterbacks coach Steve Mariucci said after the game. "He was like Michael Jordan when he was hitting all of those threes and couldn't believe they were going in."

Favre's performance was so great the Bears angrily objected to him receiving accolades for playing hurt.

"That's a bunch of bull," linebacker Vinson Smith said.

"I didn't believe it when I first heard it early in the week. I still don't believe it. It's something they cooked up."

The Bears game, and all the legend that goes with it, vaulted Favre into the national spotlight. And when he followed that game with nine touchdown passes in his next three games, giving him 14 in four games with just one interception, he became an instant MVP candidate. Favre had put together four straight games of 100-plus passer rating despite still being hobbled by the ankle injury.

In retrospect, the injury might have been a turning point in his career. It forced him to abandon the wild, gun-slinger ways of his past and sit in the pocket and run the offense the way it was supposed to be run.

"It kind of slows down the game," Detmer said. "You don't feel like you can move around as much and make things happen, so it forces you to go through your progressions and be more aware of the timing of the routes and those kinds of things.

"Brett's never been a model for footwork, and those things and that injury kind of slowed him down where his feet were more under control and it factored into all that."

The Packers finished the season 11-5 and won their first NFC Central Division title since 1972. The season-finale against Pittsburgh solidified Favre's standing as one of the toughest quarterbacks around when he twice had the wind knocked out of him, the second time causing him to cough up blood and suffer a concussion.

The Packers went on to shock the San Francisco 49ers in the playoffs in one of the most memorable games of the Favre era, and in the NFC Championship Game, Favre threw for 307 yards and three touchdowns in a 38-27 loss to the Dallas Cowboys.

The best was still yet to come, but already Favre was being welcomed into an elite club, even if he never acknowledged it to anyone else.

"Brett never really changed the whole time I was around him," Detmer said. "He enjoyed playing and messing around in the locker room. He seems to be the same type of guy now. We had a pretty solid team around him to keep him humble. It was a lot of fun, a fun group of guys. Everyone was tuned in to what we were trying to do." ❹

Gary Porter

DRUG ABUSE ROCKS HIS WORLD

Dependence on painkillers brings him to a new low in his career with Packers

By Gary D'Amato

On the afternoon of May 14, 1996, Brett Favre stepped to the podium in the Lambeau Field auditorium and dozens of reporters assembled for a scheduled news conference knew immediately that something was wrong.

Favre was wearing a sports coat instead of the T-shirt and sweaty baseball cap that had long defined him sartorially. Furthermore, he was flanked by his future wife, Deanna Tynes, and a very sober-looking Mike Holmgren, head coach of the Green Bay Packers.

Then the words came out, haltingly and in a trembling tone.

Favre, 26, who just months earlier had led the Packers to within one game of the Super Bowl, had voluntarily entered the league's substance-abuse program and would seek help at an inpatient treatment facility. He said he had "possibly become dependent upon medication."

Favre sat in his cubicle in the Packers' locker room one day in October 2005 and shook his head at the memory of that May day mayday.

"I look back at that time, almost 10 years ago, and think, 'Did that really happen?'" he said, rubbing his closely cropped hair. "It almost seems like it wasn't part of my life,

or it was a different part of my life."

Or maybe it's just that his life turned out to be so different.

No longer the self-described wild thing who "drank up Atlanta" as a rookie with the Falcons in 1991 and brought the party with him to Green Bay in '92, Favre is, by all accounts, a devoted husband to Deanna and doting father to daughters Brittany and Breleigh.

Once an indefatigable man about town, Favre now lives a near-reclusive lifestyle, according to his friends, and shuns an adoring but intrusive public whenever possible. The future Hall of Fame quarterback prefers to lie low at his palatial house on the outskirts of Hattiesburg, Miss., where he almost obsessively tends to his emerald lawn.

In 2005, Scott Favre said his younger brother quit drinking alcohol "six or seven years ago," but he remembers the good ol' days, which, in hindsight, weren't all that good.

"When we drank, it was all or nothing," Scott said. "If we drank, let's go get a case and go till we can't go no more. We were out of control. Couldn't see it at the time. Now we look back at it – and Brett and I talk about it all the time – quitting is the best thing we ever did."

Team physician Patrick McKenzie attends to Favre after he injured his ankle during a 27-24 loss at Minnesota in 1995.

The Favres didn't touch alcohol while growing up near tiny Kiln, Miss. They didn't dare, because their father, Irvin, also was their high school football coach and would have cracked his boys' skulls had he smelled beer on their breath.

After Brett Favre went away to the University of Southern Mississippi on a football scholarship, however, things changed quickly. As a 17-year-old freshman nursing a massive hangover, he came off the bench to lead the Golden Eagles to a come-from-behind victory over Tulane and became the starter.

Favre drank beer throughout his college years, frequently to excess.

"I hate to say (coach Curley Hallman) turned a blind eye to it," said Chris Ryals, Favre's roommate, "but maybe the rules were stretched just a little bit for Brett on occasion where they wouldn't be for somebody else.

"We were playing down at (Louisiana) Lafayette and we had a few beers in our motel room the night before the game. Curley asked me after the season, 'Was Brett's daddy in the room down there with y'all?' I said, 'No, sir, why?' He said, 'When we checked out we saw they charged y'all's room six beers.'

"I just smiled. So Curley Hallman kind of knew."

Favre enhanced his reputation as the life of the party in Atlanta, where Falcons coach Jerry Glanville quickly tired of his undisciplined quarterback's antics and was not disappointed when the team traded him to the Packers.

Though Favre started taking football seriously in Green Bay, he continued to play as hard off the field as he did on it.

The beginning of his transformation can be traced to Nov. 15, 1992, when he suffered a separated left shoulder while being sacked by, of all people, Reggie White, who played for the Philadelphia Eagles then but would eventually help Favre lead the Packers to victory in Super Bowl XXXI.

Favre had replaced an injured Don Majkowski just eight weeks earlier and didn't want Holmgren to know how badly he was hurt. After the game, which Green Bay won, 27-24, Favre asked the team doctor for a painkiller.

That night, he took his first Vicodin.

The powerful narcotic analgesic was distributed cautiously by the team physicians, one or at most two at a time, because of the potential for addiction. The players called the huge pills "vikes."

"Some players take it and get sick to their stomach, so they don't do it again," Favre wrote in his 1997 autobiography "Favre: For the Record." "Other players think it feels pretty good but they'd never take it enough to get addicted. Then there are players like me, who take it and get hooked."

Favre soothed various aches and pains with Vicodin throughout the 1992 and '93 seasons. By the end of the '94 season, however, he was popping six pills a day, which soon became eight, then 10, then 15.

He got the pills, he wrote, from unwitting teammates who offered up their own modest supplies when the likable quarterback confided that his shoulder hurt or his ankle was sore or his ribs were killing him. No one guessed Favre was fast developing a dangerous dependency.

He was plagued by many of the drug's side effects. He was constantly dehydrated, acutely constipated – he often went a week or longer between bowel movements – and endured bouts of nausea and vomiting. He choked down the pills at precisely 9 each night and when they kicked in, he was so wired up he paced the house or played video games until the early morning hours, while an increasingly suspicious Deanna slept fitfully upstairs.

Sometimes, he would vomit up the pills, then carefully wash them off and force them down again.

Favre's agent, James "Bus" Cook, began to suspect his star client had a problem. Favre wrote that one of his best friends, Clark Henegan, told him bluntly, "Man, you've got to stop with the pills. It's gone too far."

A few weeks after Favre led the Packers to the 1995 NFC Championship Game – and threw three touchdown passes in a 38-27 loss to the Dallas Cowboys – he decided to quit Vicodin cold turkey. He polished off his stash of 15 pills and flushed the bottle down the toilet.

But his nightmare was just beginning.

In February 1996, Favre flew to Green Bay to have bone chips removed from his left ankle. After surgery, he was sitting up in his hospital bed, talking to Deanna, when he suffered a seizure. His eyes rolled back in his head, his arms and legs thrashed and his body stiffened. Brittany, who was

Karen Sherlock

Favre and head coach Mike Holmgren speak at a July 1996 news conference in Green Bay after Favre completed his rehabilitation at the Menninger Clinic in Kansas. On several occasions, Holmgren used a hand-on-shoulder technique to advise his star quarterback not to answer particular questions about his stay in the drug treatment center.

in the room, asked Deanna, "Is he going to die, Mommy?"

The cause of the seizure was debatable, but the fact is seizures are one possible side effect of Vicodin. It was a wake-up call for Favre, who agreed to meet with NFL-appointed doctors at the urging of the Packers' medical personnel.

According to Favre's autobiography, the meeting took place in Chicago in March 1996. The league doctors asked him a lot of questions about his alcohol use. Finally, one of them said, "We know you're addicted to painkillers and we think you have a drinking problem, too."

They suggested Favre seek treatment at the Menninger Clinic in Topeka, Kan. He got up and walked out of the room.

The NFL doctors kept calling. Favre kept ignoring them. Finally, a league doctor called and said Favre had been classified as behavioral-referred instead of self-referred because the Packers' team doctors had contacted the NFL about his addiction to painkillers.

Now, Favre had no choice. He had to report to the

Menninger Clinic or he would be fined four weeks' pay, or about $900,000.

It was time for Favre to let Holmgren and Packers general manager Ron Wolf in on his secret. They were stunned by their quarterback's admission that he had a problem with painkillers. Holmgren suggested Favre address the media, and on May 14 the team issued an 11-paragraph news release and Favre found himself standing before reporters who had mostly chronicled his meteoric rise.

"The hardest thing I've ever done was stand up there," Favre said in October 2005. "It wasn't just the media I was telling. It was basically the whole world."

On June 28, 1996, Favre completed a 46-day stay at the Menninger Clinic, where he checked his celebrity status at the door, attended group therapy sessions and was evaluated by a psychiatrist. While he was in Topeka, coming to grips with his addiction, he proposed to Deanna, and they were married in July, just before the start of training camp.

Early in camp, trim and fit, Favre addressed the media in the same team auditorium where he had made his halting admission nine weeks earlier. This time his face had color, his voice was strong and he oozed confidence.

"Believe me when I tell you that this is going to be hard, but I have faced tougher trials and succeeded," he said. "I will not allow myself to be defeated by this challenge."

He also denied rumors he was an alcoholic, though he would have to abstain from alcohol for two years in order to comply with the league's substance-abuse program and eventually would quit drinking altogether. Ignoring Holmgren's jabs under the table, Favre set his jaw and vowed to take the Packers to the Super Bowl, challenging his detractors to "bet against me."

Six months later, Green Bay beat New England, 35-21, in Super Bowl XXXI at the Superdome in New Orleans, just 45 miles from Favre's hometown.

Over the ensuing years, while he established himself as one of the greatest quarterbacks of all time, Favre suffered several significant injuries and each time treated his pain with over-the-counter pain relievers, such as Tylenol. Vicodin remained in his past, a distant memory from "another life." ❹

HAVING THE TIME OF HIS LIFE

Favre puts it all together during title season

By Bob McGinn

Since he was a little boy playing in the bayous of Mississippi, Brett Favre had been taught by his football-coaching father what it took to win, what it meant to win and how wonderful it was to win.

Neither fame nor fortune could ever dull Favre's almost child-like zeal to compete in the sport that he loved most.

Given that context, it should be obvious what Favre regards as the zenith of his years with the Green Bay Packers. That would be Jan. 26, 1997, the day at the Louisiana Superdome when Favre and his teammates defeated the New England Patriots, 35-21, to win Super Bowl XXXI.

"It's the most important thing," Favre said in October 2005. "It's easy at this point in my career to look past that because I've won one. Think of the guys who haven't won one. I'm fortunate to have been on a team that won one."

The great Dan Marino made it to the Super Bowl in his second season, lost and never played in another. Dan Fouts, Warren Moon and Archie Manning never made it at all.

Those '96 Packers were the product of shrewd management, brilliant coaching and outstanding personnel. They led the National Football League in most points scored (456) and fewest points allowed (210); the undefeated Miami Dolphins of 1972 had been the last team to accomplish the feat. No team has done it since.

In the playoffs, the Packers throttled the San Francisco 49ers, the Carolina Panthers and the Patriots by a combined score of 100-48.

In 19 games, their turnover differential was plus-24.

"The team that (Ron) Wolf put together and (Mike) Holmgren coached in 1996 was quite possibly the best single-season NFL team since the great 15-1 Bears team that went on to destroy the Patriots in Super Bowl XX," the late Joel Buchsbaum wrote in Pro Football Weekly six months after the Packers' return to glory.

The strength of that team was a defense with no weak links as masterminded by Fritz Shurmur. Incomparable Reggie White anchored a front four that also included stalwarts Gilbert Brown, Santana Dotson and Sean Jones. Linebackers Brian Williams, Wayne Simmons and George Koonce were rugged and reliable. LeRoy Butler was the finest safety in the game, Eugene Robinson was a sage at free safety, cornerbacks Craig Newsome and Doug Evans had strong seasons and rookie Tyrone Williams was a superb nickel back.

Desmond Howard had five returns for touchdowns in

The little boy of joy in Favre can't be contained after his TD pass to Antonio Freeman in Super Bowl XXXI.

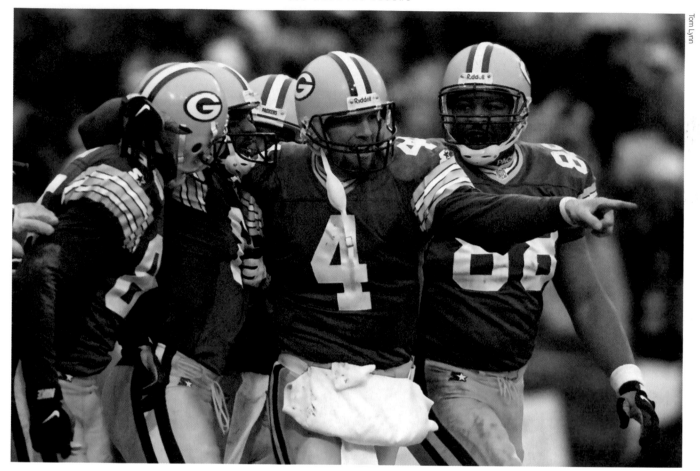

Tom Lynn

Favre celebrates a third-quarter touchdown pass to Andre Rison (second from left), with Antonio Freeman (left) and Keith Jackson (88) during their game against the Minnesota Vikings in December 1996 at Lambeau Field. The Packers won the game, 38-10.

the 19 games, Craig Hentrich's punts and kickoffs were high and deep, and place-kicker Chris Jacke generally was money in the bank.

Still, this was a club that lost games on the road against Minnesota in Week 4, Kansas City in Week 10 and Dallas in Week 11, and in each Green Bay essentially was dominated.

What can be forgotten about those championship Packers were the many problems that the offense encountered during the season. At times, the unit floundered. Favre was sacked 40 times in the regular season, most in his career, as the Packers ranked merely 18th in percentage of sacks allowed. Decimated by injury, the receiving corps was overmatched a time or two.

But the Packers always had Favre.

He could turn disaster into a touchdown. With him, the remarkable became routine. Most of all, no matter how poor his protection was or who was lining up at wide receiver, he led this team every step of the way with a burning desire to win.

"I think he's taken a lot of this on his shoulders to get us there," offensive coordinator Sherman Lewis said after the NFC Championship Game rout of Carolina. "I think he was under a lot of pressure. I think he put it on himself. He doesn't shy away from that."

Instead, Favre tackled adversity head-on. And the entire organization fed off his unbridled optimism, toughness and will to win.

"We have the best quarterback in football," his mentor,

Tom Lynn

Holmgren, said after one midseason game. "If he has time to throw the ball, we think we can get most things done."

His thirst for a Super Bowl ring was one of two primal forces driving Favre in 1996. The other was his determination to prove beyond a shadow of a doubt that he could play just as well if not better than in his MVP season of 1995 despite his addiction to the pain-killing drug Vicodin.

On June 28, Favre completed a 46-day stay at a rehabilitation center in Kansas. On July 14, he married Deanna Tynes, whom he had been dating for 12 years. And, on July 17, he sat next to the protective Holmgren at a news conference in which he said: "You know I'm going to beat this thing. I'm going to the Super Bowl. All I can tell people is if they don't believe me, just bet against me."

Favre had lost weight at the Menninger Clinic but none of his incredible arm strength and explosive abilities. He was fast and could really run at age 27, and with him making

Favre often ran away from defenders early in his career. Here, he stiff-arms Eagles linebacker James Willis in September 1996 in Green Bay. The Packers won the game 39-13.

athletic play after athletic play the Packers broke from the chute by crushing Tampa Bay (34-3), a Philadelphia team that would finish 10-6 (39-13) and San Diego (42-10).

"Favre is unconscious right now," Detroit pro scout Rick Spielman said at halftime of the Eagles game. "The way he improvises and finds open receivers . . . he's the best quarterback in the league right now. No one comes close."

Even in the early victories, the pass-rush pressure had been intense, but Favre just ran away from it. But the next week in Minnesota the tidal wave of Purple proved too much. Gary Brown, the left tackle, was responsible for two of the seven sacks, two major penalties, four knockdowns

Rick Wood

Tom Lynn

(left) Favre is sacked in November 1996 in a 27-20 loss at Kansas City. (above) Andre Rison hauls in a 54-yard touchdown pass from Favre in the Super Bowl in January 1997. Rison beat Patriots cornerback Otis Smith for the first score in the game. Favre changed the play at the line of scrimmage when he detected a blitz. He called it the best audible of his career.

and seven hurries. Center Frank Winters, left guard Aaron Taylor and rookie right guard Adam Timmerman also struggled. Only right tackle Earl Dotson held up.

Never one to chastise teammates, Favre said after the carnage was over, "I don't know if anyone in this room thought we would go 16-0. So here it is. Now you go on."

Brown would make five starts, Ken Ruettgers one (before retiring Nov. 20 with degenerative knee problems) and John Michels nine before old pro Bruce Wilkerson was summoned to stanch the leakage in Week 16 and the playoffs.

The woes at wide receiver began in Week 7 when Robert Brooks suffered a season-ending knee injury. A week later, Antonio Freeman was crunched making a catch and broke his left forearm. In Week 10, tight end Mark Chmura went

Tom Lynn

(left) Favre celebrates with LeRoy Butler after his fourth touchdown pass during a 28-18 victory over Detroit on Nov. 3, 1996. Favre connected with Don Beebe on the 65-yard pass. Favre said of Butler: "He was a great player and a great teammate, and no one had as much fun as LeRoy." (above) Reggie White gives Favre a hug after their 23-20 overtime victory over San Francisco in a Monday night game in October 1996 at Lambeau Field.

down with a sprained arch.

Wolf tried to nickel-and-dime it for a few weeks by signing veteran Anthony Morgan to join Don Beebe, Terry Mickens and rookie Derrick Mayes. But when nobody could get open for Favre in Dallas, the Packers hurriedly put in a waiver claim the next day for Andre Rison.

The next Sunday night in St. Louis, Favre had to spend most of the game telling Rison what to do coming out of the huddle. Trailing by nine points late in the first half, Favre then helped rally the troops for a critical 24-9 victory.

Freeman and Chmura were back by December, the offensive line jelled and Favre kicked it into high gear. In the final seven games, his passer ratings were 108.7, 89.9,

Jeffrey Phelps

(opposite) Favre pauses after being hit very late in the fourth quarter in yet another loss in Dallas, this one 21-6 in November 1996. (above) A Packers staff member cleans Favre's cleats during a 1996 game at Lambeau Field.

92.1, 132.6, 107.4, 107.3 and 107.9.

"If this had happened my first year and I had lost Sterling (Sharpe) I would have been lost," Favre said. "But I'm to a point now where I can go to running backs, tight ends and backup receivers."

A few days before the divisional playoff game, the Associated Press announced its MVP award. Given his stay in rehabilitation and what he perceived as an army of doubters, Favre desperately wanted to win again. In a runaway, it was Favre with 52 votes from a nationwide panel of writers, followed by John Elway with 33 $^1/_2$, Terrell Davis with 5 $^1/_2$ and Jerome Bettis with 2.

"This is like a big weight was lifted off my shoulders," Favre said. "Now it's like, 'Whew! Now I can just relax.'"

Chmura remembered how amped Favre was throughout the post-season. After watching fans at Lambeau Field

"Favre is unconscious right now. ... He's the best quarterback in the league right now. No one comes close."

Rick Spielman,
then Detroit pro scout, during the Packers' victory over the Eagles in Week 2 of 1996

weep with joy after the frigid triumph over Carolina, Favre said: "To go without a Super Bowl leaves an empty feeling for me and for my team. I don't think anybody can stop us, I really don't."

Playing in New Orleans almost was like a home game for Favre, but there was pressure as well. Busloads of reporters made the pilgrimage to Kiln, Miss., scouring his hometown for dirt and details. None other than Bill Belichick, the Patriots' nonpareil defensive coach, had two weeks to solve the mystery of stopping Favre.

On the Packers' second play from scrimmage, Belichick brought a six-man blitz. Before he could do so, Favre recognized it and made what he says was the best audible of his career.

"The play was 322 Y Stick, just a little dump-off to the tight end," Favre recalled in 2004. "I said, 'Black 78 Razor.' Black meant we're changing it. 78 was the protection. It was a two-man route. Razor means Z (flanker) runs a post and X (split end) runs a shake."

Lined up wide to the right, Rison beat cornerback Otis Smith at the line and caught Favre's perfect throw 33 yards downfield. The Patriots' secondary blew a call so there was no safety in the middle of the field. The result was a 54-yard touchdown and a launching pad for victory.

"I've done everything I possibly can," Favre said in a joyous locker room. "I hope too many people didn't bet against me because they're broke right now." ❹

Jim Gehrz

Rick Wood

Mark Gail

(left) Favre shows his delight after Antonio Freeman recovered Edgar Bennett's goal-line fumble for a touchdown in the third quarter of a 35-14 divisional playoff victory against San Francisco on Jan. 4, 1997, at Lambeau Field. (top) Teammate Reggie White embraces Favre on the podium after defeating New England in Super Bowl XXXI in 1997 in New Orleans. "We will go as far as Brett can take us," White had said before the start of that season. (above) Mechanics? What mechanics? Favre, noted for his unconventional throws, gets off a pass against the Patriots.

(left) Steve Hoffman, then 8, with his dad, Paul Hoffman, were two of the lucky ones to get an autograph signed by Favre after practice in July 1997. At the time, eight Packers signed autographs for fans after each morning practice and this was Favre's day to sign. The Hoffmans were from Manitowoc, Wis. (above) Sweet: Favre and Reggie White had candy bars named after them after the Packers' victory in Super Bowl XXXI.

YEAR OF GREAT HIGHS, LOWS

Favre's fabulous season ends with bitter defeat

By Bob McGinn

At the beginning, the headline read, "Favre Lands the Big One."

At the end, the headline might have read, "Packers, Favre Lose the Big One."

Such was 1997 for Brett Favre, a year in which he would once again reach the mountaintop for personal achievement in the National Football League but also fall agonizingly short in the Green Bay Packers' quest for victory in a second straight Super Bowl.

Basking in the afterglow of Super Bowl XXXI and his second Associated Press Most Valuable Player award, Favre was larger than life.

In April, plans were announced to open Brett Favre Steakhouse on Water Street in Milwaukee. In June, his galleries at the Vince Lombardi Memorial Golf Classic in suburban Milwaukee dwarfed those of the 54 other celebrities. In July, he signed a seven-year, $47.25 million contract that contained a $12 million signing bonus.

Then there was the day in early June on a small lake outside Minocqua in Vilas County when Favre aimlessly threw his second cast out of the boat while taping a commercial and fishing show. Using equipment normally associated with walleye fishing, Favre landed a 36-inch, full-bodied musky, the Holy Grail for Wisconsin anglers.

"Talk about a guy who has the magic touch," said Joe Sweeney, Favre's marketing agent at the time. "And the funny thing is, Brett doesn't understand how big this is."

Packermania was off the charts in the summer of '97. Safety LeRoy Butler opened training camp by saying the team's realistic goal was to run the table as undefeated champions, a 19-0 feat that Favre declared to be "highly possible" on the eve of the regular season.

Huckster Michael Buffer's "Let's get ready to rrruuummmbbblllle!" greeted the Lambeau Field crowd that was beside itself for the Monday night opener against the Chicago Bears.

The Packers managed to repulse the Bears but weren't so lucky the next Sunday in Philadelphia. Blitzed into submission by coach Ray Rhodes, Favre was down on the rock-hard artificial turf at Veterans Stadium 12 times in a 10-9 defeat.

Philadelphia was the first of at least seven opponents that decided to throw the book at Favre and an ordinary offensive line for which right guard Adam Timmerman was the only 19-game starter. The last team that attempted wholesale blitzing, the underdog Denver Broncos, ultimately won Super Bowl XXXII because of it.

In Week 3, Favre sent the Miami Dolphins home as a 23-18 loser by running away from four point-blank sacks that left

Denver's Neil Smith prances after recovering a fumble by Favre during the second quarter of Super Bowl XXXII on Jan. 25, 1998, in San Diego.

Dale Guldan

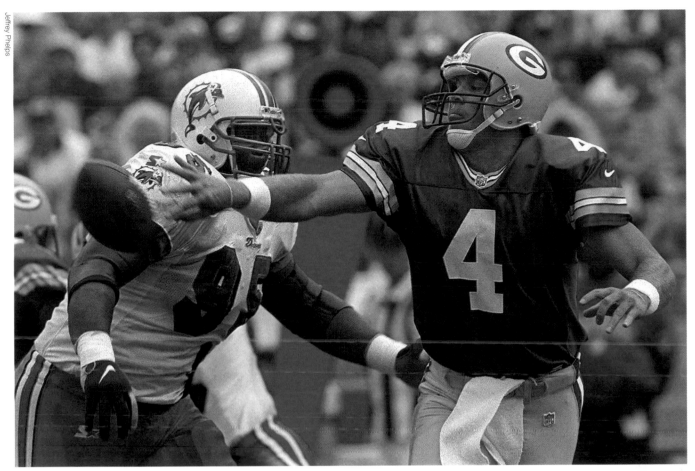

Jeffrey Phelps

(opposite) **Favre scuffles with Vikings linebacker Jeff Brady, a former Packer, on Sept. 21, 1997. The Packers won, 38-32. (above) Despite pressure from Miami's Tim Bowens, Favre completes a pass in a game in September 1997.**

coach Jimmy Johnson incredulous. In Week 4, Favre was brilliant with five touchdown passes, each of which required tremendous velocity, in a 38-32 victory over Minnesota.

"I thought we rattled him an awful lot," Vikings linebackers coach Tom Olivadotti said. "He just got away. We were in his face and he made some great throws. Some great throws."

Early in his sixth season, Favre already was surpassing some club records. The five touchdowns against the Vikings gave him 156, surpassing Bart Starr's total of 152 in 16 years.

Favre's capacity to turn would-be sacks into huge plays became a common theme throughout the season. Part of the reason Favre was so hard to sack was the 237 pounds that he was carrying, up 25 from late '96.

"I'm moving around better and I'm able to shed tacklers," said Favre, who made it through another season taking every snap that counted. "I'm able to throw with people hanging onto me. I feel much better than last year."

The Packers were 3-1 heading to the Silverdome in late September. They left with a 3-2 record and trailing Tampa Bay by two games in the NFC Central Division, four more injured players on offense and Favre so mortified by what easily turned out to be his worst game of the season that he couldn't bear facing reporters after the 26-15 defeat.

From the Department of Unforgettable, there was the second-quarter play when Favre stumbled coming out from center. From his knees, he rifled a pass that was intercepted at point-blank range by linebacker Reggie Brown and brought back 45 yards for a score.

Mark Hoffman

Mark Hoffman

(opposite) "Brett, don't!" could be heard in living rooms across Packer Nation when Favre prepared to throw from his knees against Detroit in September 1997. The result? A 45-yard interception return for a touchdown by the Lions' Reggie Brown (above). The Lions won, 26-15, in the Silverdome.

"In the archives, I'm sure you could find somebody who did that," Favre's red-faced coach, Mike Holmgren, said. "I don't think it's a great thing to do. Bad things happen."

But Favre wasn't down for long. In a showdown the next week with the Buccaneers, Favre got into Billy Schroeder's face after a dropped pass and the Packers won, 21-16.

Two defensive-minded head coaches, Chicago's Dave Wannstedt and New England's Pete Carroll, plus autonomous defensive coordinators Larry Peccatiello of

Detroit and Bud Carson of St. Louis all failed in the next four weeks to stop Favre and a ground game spearheaded by Dorsey Levens that would average 119.3 yards, best in Green Bay since '85.

Then the unthinkable happened. A 13-point favorite against Lindy Infante and the winless Indianapolis Colts, the Packers lost, 41-38, even though Favre was terrific.

"We lost three games that year and we really didn't need to lose any," Favre said in October 2005. "We were in better shape injury-wise than in '96 and that was the most confident team I ever played on. We were never out of a game. We were so good, at times it may have worked against us."

What followed was a stretch of five games in which Favre defeated Dallas for the first time, won his first game at the Metrodome, helped clinch the division title in a 17-6 victory in Tampa and sliced and diced both Carolina and Buffalo.

The Tampa Bay game was most notable. Playing at the old stadium for the last time, the Packers had a one-game lead in the NFC Central standings. With a sellout throng at full throat, Favre was able to assert his presence and talent over the entire assembly despite minimal help from his teammates and thwart an intelligent, No. 3-ranked defense masterminded by Monte Kiffin, perhaps the leading coordinator of his generation.

In that first half, which ended with the Packers leading by a point, the Packers were afflicted by two lost fumbles, a dropped bomb by Robert Brooks, touchback-type punting by Craig Hentrich, uncharacteristic clock mismanagement and a botched field-goal try.

The game, a 17-6 victory, is one of which Favre has no recollection, but he should. On his first touchdown pass, he scrambled against a stiff rush and, about 1 yard from the line, spotted Brooks running free through the middle of the secondary for a 43-yard score. On the second, a third and 2 from the 8, Favre ran up again and a split-second before crossing the line and being crushed by Warren Sapp flipped a side-armed pass to Levens at the 2.

In what was becoming almost a typical performance, Favre completed 25 of 33 passes with three throwaways, two drops, one pass broken up, one off line and one interception.

"Brett is able to control the game, and this season he's doing it so well," Holmgren said. "I don't know what else we could ask of Brett Favre."

Jeffrey Phelps

Favre evades a sack by Detroit linebacker Reggie Brown in a 20-10 Packers victory Nov. 2, 1997.

When the ballots of 48 writers were counted, Favre and Detroit's Barry Sanders each had 18 votes to share AP MVP honors. Sanders rushed for 2,053 yards, second-most in NFL history, and became just the sixth back to average more than 6 yards per carry (6.13). Favre had carried Green Bay to another 13-3 season despite an unsettled line and the failure of secondary receivers to emerge.

"The more I've thought about it, the more excited I am about it," Favre said. "Sure, I'd like to win it out-right, but I'm sharing it with probably the best running back to ever play the game."

Favre remains not only the only player to win the award three times in a row but also the only player to win it three times. Period.

After dispatching Tampa Bay for a third time, Favre was matched against the San Francisco 49ers' top-rated defense on the West Coast in the NFC Championship Game.

Oblivious to wind, rain and mud, Favre played mistake-free football against a blitzing defense, posted a passer rating of 98.1 and directed a 23-10 triumph.

As he was wont to do, Favre inserted his own priceless sense of humor in the tense battle. On fourth and 1, Favre tried long and hard with his cadence to get San Francisco's front four to jump. With the jig up and a few seconds left on the play clock, he bent down and chatted with defensive tackle Dana Stubblefield as if to say, "Won't you please jump offside?"

Some thought the Super Bowl might be anti-climactic after the Packers' dominating show against the top-seeded 49ers. An 11½-point underdog, the wild-card Broncos had different ideas.

Certainly, the Packers' season-long inability to stop the run was a killer. So, too, was Holmgren's bad week climaxed by his losing track of the down and then letting Terrell Davis score the winning touchdown.

As for Favre, his performance deserved a "C" when he needed to bring his "B-plus" or "A" game against a Greg Robinson-coordinated defense that all-out blitzed to an incredible degree. In 2007, Ron Wolf placed the blame for the defeat squarely on Holmgren. Years earlier, two unidentified coaches had informed the retired general manager that Holmgren stubbornly had refused to make what should have been rather routine early adjustments.

According to Holmgren, Favre gambled and lost on a first-quarter interception and a second-quarter fumble, both of which led to Denver touchdowns.

"We practiced everything they threw at us," Holmgren said a few months after the 31-24 defeat. "And we went over them many times with Brett. We told him, no matter what, when you see them coming, get the ball out of there. Don't hold onto it to make the big play. There were many times he didn't do that in the game, and it cost us. He saw

(top) Favre follows William Henderson to run for a first down at Minnesota in a Monday night game in December 1997. The Packers won, 27-11. (left) Favre hoists the George Halas Trophy after Green Bay beat San Francisco in the NFC Championship Game on Jan. 11, 1998, at 3Com Park. Favre was saying "Mine" as he did this.

Jeffrey Phelps

(opposite) Favre eludes a tackle by Denver's John Mobley during Super Bowl XXXII on Jan. 25, 1998, in San Diego. (above) Favre is on the ground after his pass was picked off in the first quarter of the 31-24 Super Bowl loss to Denver.

it coming and didn't pay any attention to it."

When told that Holmgren had pushed some of the blame onto Favre, tight end Mark Chmura said in 2005, "That's a flat-out lie. How can you get rid of the ball when the receiver is running a 15- or 20-yard in or dig? You can't scream to him and tell him, 'Blitz!' We weren't a sight blitz team. The receivers weren't responsible for seeing if there's a blitz and breaking their route off accordingly. That's a bunch of crap."

In October 2005, Favre maintained that the Packers had never practiced against the Broncos' weak-corner or weak-safety blitzes, which today are common. He said Holmgren did make adjustments in the second half.

"If we had had those protections earlier in the game..." Favre said, failing to finish his thought. The Packers started drives from their 48, 11 and 30 in the final 11 minutes but failed to score. Antonio Freeman dropped a pass at the Denver 15 with 40 seconds left, the first of three straight incompletions as the Packers' final drive flickered and died.

"When I think of the two Super Bowls, I think more of the one we won but I probably dwell more on the Denver game," Favre said in 2005. "I don't think we underestimated Denver. We still got to the Super Bowl. We lost to a damn good Denver team. I think everyone realized the following year how good they were." ❹

Lots of attention for an ol' country boy: Favre talks to reporters at media day in San Diego for Super Bowl XXXII.

Dale Guldan

FORMIDABLE RELATIONSHIP ENDS

Holmgren leaves for Seattle after '98 season

By Lori Nickel

The man who would mold Brett Favre into a three-time MVP, help get him his only championship ring, have more of an influence on him than any other man except his own father . . .

Well, that man would leave him.

Favre couldn't believe it, though, until Green Bay Packers coach Mike Holmgren was finally on an airplane headed for Seattle after the 1998 season.

"Everyone talked about him leaving. I said, 'You're crazy,' " Favre recalled in 2005. "I was so naïve. The year before, at the Super Bowl we lost, that week, all the press conferences, they asked the question to me: what I thought about Mike Holmgren possibly leaving. I thought it was the stupidest question I'd ever heard. First time I'd ever heard it. I thought that question was odd, off the wall, and forgot about it.

"Well, a year later, he left, and I just expected us to be together forever."

Looking back, the 1998 season began what would be one of many great tests for Favre. It was one of many transitions he would have to make throughout his career.

The Packers had the shortest off-season possible, having wrapped up the 1997 season with a loss to Denver in the Super Bowl. They then began '98 six months later with an extra exhibition game halfway around the world in Tokyo.

The Packers finished with an 11-5 record in 1998 and lost in the first round of the playoffs at San Francisco.

After winning an unprecedented three straight Most Valuable Player awards, Favre led the league with 4,212 passing yards and 347 completions, and threw 31 touchdown passes in 1998. Yet he would not even get to the Pro Bowl. Randall Cunningham, Steve Young and Chris Chandler, all with better quarterback ratings, went instead.

But that year is memorable for the people close to Favre who left at the end of the season, especially Holmgren.

The Packers started the regular season in a way that had become typical for them – winning. They beat Detroit, Tampa Bay, Cincinnati and Carolina, and in that time, little went wrong.

"It's nice to have the best quarterback in football on your side," Holmgren said in that stretch. "He has such a good grasp of what we're doing now."

Head coach Mike Holmgren embraces Favre after Green Bay wins another NFC Central Division title with a 17-7 victory over Tampa Bay in December 1997 in Tampa.

Rick Wood

Tom Lynn

(opposite) Favre greets Eagles coach Andy Reid after the Eagles beat the Packers, 47-17, in December 2004 in Philadelphia. (above) A dejected Packers head coach Mike Holmgren leaves the field after the 49ers defeated Green Bay, 30-27, in the playoffs Jan. 3, 1999, in San Francisco. It was his final game as coach of the Packers.

But the Packers' 29-game home winning streak (regular season and playoffs) ended in Week 5 when Minnesota, led by rookie receiver Randy Moss' two touchdowns, controlled both sides of the ball and won, 37-24.

Still, in seven years, Holmgren would have a 47-5 record at Lambeau Field. He preached the necessity to win at home to ease the pressure of winning on the road. Back in those days, from 1996-'98, the Packers would play three consecutive road games in a season, so Holmgren felt he had to lock up Lambeau.

"He and Ron Wolf had a lot to do with winning here," Favre said in 2005. "There's no way you could not give credit to those two guys. Yeah, we had good teams, but those teams had to be put together by someone and then they had to play to a certain level, which we did.

"Mike expressed to us, it's difficult to go out and win on the road, and we will do it, but you're better off winning at home first. If you can go 8-0 at home, you're OK to lose some on the road, and we did that. Now I understand what

"He and Mike had a unique relationship. They respected the heck out of each other, but they were very similar in a lot of ways. ...both of them are very competitive."

Andy Reid,
Philadelphia Eagles coach who was Favre's quarterbacks coach in 1997 and 1998

he was talking about."

Meanwhile, as the touchdowns and yards were piling up as usual for Favre, in Week 4 his game hit the skids. He threw three interceptions at Carolina, three against Minnesota, three at Detroit, two against Baltimore and three against San Francisco. From Sept. 27 to Nov. 1, "that was a pretty rough time," Andy Reid said in November 2005. The coach of the Philadelphia Eagles now, Reid was Favre's quarterbacks coach at the time.

"That was not a good time in particular for Brett and for Brett's coach," Reid said. "But the thing we figured was, if he kept firing, and without hesitation, he was going to be OK. He did. He's probably a lot like a jump-shooter like Michael Jordan or Larry Bird, or the great ones today. One wants those guys to keep shooting, work their way through it. That's the approach we took with Brett."

Favre deflected the unwanted criticism by playing pranks in the locker room. He stuffed a Milky Way candy bar into his mouth before his news conference when he said he couldn't find one of his own chocolate bars that were everywhere in Green Bay. He tried to keep his sense of humor.

"Everyone is wondering, what's wrong with Brett Favre?" he said in his news conference at the time. "I'm getting sick of hearing it. The only person that I'm safe around is me. I don't even call home no more. My dad's like, 'What the hell are you doing?'

"How about a little tender loving care, you know?"

Favre rebounded, especially in games at the New York Giants, at Minnesota, at Tampa Bay and against Tennessee with quarterback ratings topping 100 points and two touchdown passes for more than 60 yards.

But the Packers were swept by Minnesota that year. The

"In our team meeting the next day, he broke down and couldn't even finish his talk to us. It happened so fast. The next thing I know, he's gone."

Brett Favre,

recalling Mike Holmgren's talk the day after the Packers' loss to San Francisco in the playoffs to end the 1998 season

Jeffrey Phelps

Vikings finished 15-1 and ran away with the Central Division title.

The Packers, meanwhile, played all year with injuries. Four players started at running back, including Dorsey Levens, a Pro Bowl selection the previous season who missed 10 weeks with a broken leg and damaged ankle ligaments. Receiver Robert Brooks played hurt and on a limited basis, Derrick Mayes missed six weeks with a knee injury, and Bill Schroeder and Corey Bradford were lost for the season with injuries.

For the first time in the Holmgren era, the Packers would not win their opening playoff game.

Though San Francisco's Terrell Owens had four drops and a fumble, and the Packers had won five straight against the 49ers in the Holmgren era, the lead would change in the playoff game six times. The final change was at the very end. Steve Young's 25-yard touchdown pass to Owens with 3 seconds left enabled the Steve Mariucci-coached 49ers to stun the Packers, 30-27, in a wild-card playoff game at 3Com Park.

Favre played well, engineering an 89-yard drive to give the Packers the late 27-23 lead.

He ended the season with these grades from the Milwaukee Journal Sentinel: "Still the NFL's greatest quarterback but didn't play as well in '98. Reverted to some bad habits and forced ball into coverage on a consistent basis, leading to 25 interceptions and 84 points for opponents. All-time competitor. Makes plays with his

Seattle head coach Mike Holmgren greets Favre before their game Nov. 1, 1999, in Green Bay. On Holmgren's first trip back to Green Bay since becoming coach of the Seahawks, Seattle won, 27-7.

lethal arm and instincts that nobody else can. Everyone around him is inspired by his will to win regardless of physical price.

"NFL's 10th-ranked passer with 87.8 rating. Phenomenal leader who might be the most respected and well-liked player in the league. Grade: B-plus."

Favre was helped by a receiving corps of Antonio Freeman, Brooks, Mayes and when healthy Schroeder and Bradford. The Packers dropped merely 30 passes in 17 games, an average of 1.77 per game, the lowest drop ratio during the Holmgren years.

Favre lost others close to him in 1998. Reid got the head job with the Eagles at the end of this season, and Packers defensive great Reggie White retired, for the first time, after leading the NFC with 16 sacks and earning the Associated Press Defensive Player of the Year award. He may have been Favre's biggest fan in the locker room.

"I didn't come in here saying, 'I'm Reggie White, I've

been to the Pro Bowl seven times and I'm the man,'" White said at the time. "I came here and my whole attitude was that when we realize that No. 4 is the man, that No. 4 is the one who is going to take us and that we're going to be the supporting cast, then we're going to start winning."

But clearly, the departure of Holmgren dealt the biggest blow to Favre.

By December, the rumors of Holmgren's inevitable departure were rampant. A heckling incident at Lambeau Field by a fan got to Holmgren. As the Packers lost Jan. 3 in the playoffs, reports already had surfaced that Holmgren was headed to Seattle. They were true. Holmgren turned down an offer from Wolf that would have made him the highest-paid coach in the NFL. Six days later, Holmgren left the Packers for the omnipotence the Seahawks could give him with the titles of coach, general manager and vice president.

Favre didn't feel he could have done much to persuade Holmgren to stay.

"A lot had been made of him possibly leaving that week of San Francisco and this could be his last game with us," Favre said. "After the game, in our team meeting the next day, he broke down and couldn't even finish his talk to us. It happened so fast. The next thing I know, he's gone."

Favre said he did not at all feel betrayed by Holmgren's leaving.

"No. Absolutely not," Favre said. "I understood why he was leaving. It happened at a good time in my career because I'd had a lot of success. I knew a great deal of it was because of him and would have loved for Mike Holmgren to have stayed. I didn't feel like, OK, this is my chance to prove to people that I can play without him. That never crossed my mind. I think that was the first time in my career that my eyes were opened to, you won't be here forever. Neither will the players you play with or the coaches that coach you."

Holmgren still has great affection for Favre, a feeling that's mutual. Sometimes the two were portrayed as polar opposites, always at odds, usually with Holmgren looking steamed and Favre looking guilty. Reid often acted as the liaison between the two.

"There's probably a little of that in there," Reid said in 2005. "He and Mike had a unique relationship. They respected the heck out of each other, but they were very similar in a lot of ways. So I was kind of put in the position to mediate between the two of them a little bit, but every offensive head coach and every quarterback probably have to go through that same thing.

"Both of them are very competitive. When you're quarterback, sometimes you're going to do some things that you're going to do in a split second that maybe the coach didn't want you to do, or didn't think you should have done. They would express that to each other. But hey, they got along good. This wasn't like a bad relationship by any means. They got along well and respected each other."

Favre has mentioned Holmgren now and then with nothing but gratitude.

"We clashed, but it was a good clashing. Never ever was I mad at him," Favre said in 2005. "OK, sure I was. He was hard on me, but I knew, because I was a coach's son, and was brought up always in the shadows of football, I knew what he meant. Did I agree with it? Not always, but I knew he was right. So I just had to grin and bear it.

"I was always kind of a rebel, I guess. I was just hardheaded. And he knew it, and I always knew it, but I think my problem a lot of times is I would do it the way it was supposed to be done. But I didn't want people to know that.

"Sometimes the image of, man, he's just a gunslinger, it seems like he doesn't even study. I studied my butt off, but I didn't want people to know I was in the film room all night and all these things. But he knew. He knew that I was trying. There's no doubt in my mind that I wouldn't be here today if it wasn't for him. Because of that, I will owe him a great deal always, he and Ron Wolf both. Mike made me a better player. He called plays to put me in the right position to succeed, not once, but for seven years. I'm forever thankful for that." ❹

Mark Hoffman

NO PARTY FOR FAVRE IN 1999

Last-minute heroics, injury define season

By Gary D'Amato

Few players can last 17 years in the National Football League without experiencing some joy and misery along the way. With Brett Favre, as every Green Bay Packers fan knows, the highs have been top-of-Mount Everest stuff and the lows excruciatingly sad.

No other single season, however, can quite match the roller-coaster ride of 1999 hump for hump. No other single season so often buried the needle on Favre's emotional Richter scale.

It was a season marked alternately by joy and frustration, pain and bewilderment, individual milestones and team upheaval.

There was his battered thumb. Two-minute miracles. A humiliating loss to his former coach. The record for consecutive games played by a quarterback. A pair of ugly three-game losing streaks.

And all of it was compressed into the ill-fated 356-day tenure of Ray Rhodes as head coach of the Packers.

Ultimately, the '99 team finished with a .500 record, the benchmark of mediocrity and to that point the Packers' only non-winning season since 1992.

"We should have been better than 8-8," Favre said in 2005, and he'll get no argument from Packers fans who remember a roster loaded with the likes of Dorsey Levens,

Antonio Freeman, Robert Brooks, Gilbert Brown, LeRoy Butler and Darren Sharper.

"I'm sure Ray, if you asked him now, would take his share of the blame," Favre said. "But I look at it like everybody should take some of the blame, starting with me and all the veteran players."

Then-general manager Ron Wolf hired Rhodes on Jan. 11, 1999, to replace Mike Holmgren, who left Green Bay for Seattle just one year after taking the Packers to a second consecutive Super Bowl.

The veterans welcomed the change because Rhodes, a one-time defensive coordinator under Holmgren, had the reputation of being a "player's coach." The military environment engendered by Holmgren would be relaxed, the laundry list of nit-picky rules would be dumped, the players would be looser and therefore they would play better.

At least, that was the theory.

"If you're one minute late for a meeting, Ray won't fine you $500 or $600," Butler said after Rhodes was hired. "If you drop a pass you won't be afraid to go back to the sideline. If you drop an interception you won't be ridiculed. He won't be on you so much that you can't perform. If guys aren't relaxed, they can't perform."

Favre would be working with Sherman Lewis, the

Favre fumbles as he is hit by Minnesota cornerback Jimmy Hitchcock in December 1999. The Vikings won, 24-20.

holdover offensive coordinator who would now call the plays, a role handled previously by Holmgren. Lewis expressed his desire to use a vertical passing game and a willingness to try new things, including the shotgun formation disdained by Holmgren.

This was going to be fun.

That is, until Favre suffered what he describes as the most debilitating injury of his career. During a 27-12 loss to the Denver Broncos in an exhibition game Aug. 23, Favre smashed his right thumb on the helmet of blitzing linebacker John Mobley.

The Packers initially described the injury as minor. X-rays revealed a sprain but no broken bones. No big deal... unless you're a quarterback.

"His hand was about as fat as mine," said Santana Dotson, a 290-pound defensive tackle. "It was bad. As a quarterback, you need that opposable thumb to squeeze (the ball). That was the year I saw Brett in the training room more than any other year."

In the Packers locker room in 2005, Favre held out his hand and explained how intense pain flared from the tip to the base of his thumb and into his forefinger.

"Of all my injuries, that was the toughest," he said. "It started the exhibition game against Denver and then I reinjured it against Oakland (in the regular-season opener) and it bothered me the rest of the year, off and on. One game I'd be fine and the next, nothing.

"If you sprain an ankle, it's three weeks you hobble around and you may be limited in some ways, but you play through it. The thumb, you're getting it banged, the ball is slapping it every time you take a snap.

"It just wouldn't heal."

Despite reinjuring his thumb against Oakland, when his hand collided with the outstretched arms of defensive tackle Russell Maryland in the third quarter, Favre stayed in the game and led the Packers to a heart-stopping 28-24 victory.

Trailing by three points with 1 minute 18 seconds left, Favre drove the offense 82 yards in 11 plays for the winning touchdown. Wincing with every snap and doubling over in pain in the huddle, he somehow managed to

(above) An animated Favre speaks on the sideline with the coaching staff, including head coach Ray Rhodes, during a 27-13 loss to Dallas in November 1999 in Texas. (opposite) Favre's hand is bandaged and iced after he injured it against Denver in August 1999 in an exhibition game.

complete 6 of 7 passes for 70 yards on the drive and finished 28 for 47 for 333 yards and four touchdowns.

The emotional nature of the game — season opener, new head coach and staff, throbbing thumb, last-second victory — caused Favre to choke up during his post-game news conference. Wiping away tears, he apologized to stunned reporters and left the podium.

"After that game, I probably should have taken a week or two off," Favre later admitted.

Instead, after a loss to Detroit, Favre led the Packers to another last-second victory, 23-20, over the Minnesota

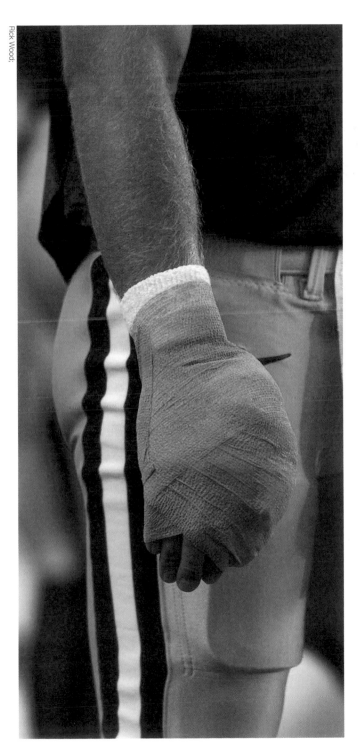

Rick Wood;

Vikings. With no timeouts left, less than 30 seconds remaining and the clock running, Favre didn't have time to call a play on fourth down from the Vikings' 23.

"He didn't even say, 'Set, hut,'" center Frank Winters said.

The three wide receivers instinctively went deep. Favre pumped right to Bill Schroeder then threw a perfect pass to Corey Bradford, who caught the ball in stride in the end zone.

Favre spent himself so much in the resulting celebration that he had to lie down on the Packers bench and receive oxygen.

"I'm too tired to cry today," he said after the game.

The next week, Favre celebrated his 30th birthday by marshaling another do-or-die touchdown drive in the final 2 minutes for a 26-23 victory over the Tampa Bay Buccaneers. This time, he threw a 21-yard pass to Freeman with 1:05 left, capping a six-play, 73-yard drive that lasted only 40 seconds.

However, the late-game heroics masked deficiencies that would come back to haunt the Packers that season. Astute football observers noted the team seemed to lack discipline. The offense was sloppy in its execution of plays and on defense the tackling was less than inspired.

At some point midway through the season, Favre remembered, Rhodes dropped the 2-minute drill from the team's practice routine despite the fact the Packers had won three of their first four games in the closing seconds.

"I remember every Thursday we worked on the 2-minute drill under (Holmgren) at the end of practice," Favre said. "I said, 'Are we going to work on 2-minute today?' Ray said, 'Nah, we're not going to work on 2-minute.' I said, 'I think we need to.' I spoke up.

"There were other times maybe I should have spoken up and the other veterans should have spoken up. But as players, you know, if you can get out of practice early...."

Some of the veterans started taking advantage of Rhodes, who talked tough but was reluctant to come down hard on his players.

"The younger guys don't know any better," Favre said. "They're going to follow what the veterans do."

The season began to unravel in Week 5, when the

Packers were throttled, 31-10, by the Denver Broncos at Mile High Stadium. The offense managed just 133 yards and Favre had one of the worst games of his career, completing 7 of 23 passes for 120 yards with three interceptions and a quarterback rating of 9.6.

After a victory at San Diego, the Packers returned home to face Holmgren and his Seattle Seahawks in a much-hyped Monday night game. Favre threw four interceptions, fumbled the ball away twice and completed just 14 of 35 passes for 180 yards in an embarrassing 27-7 defeat.

Things went from bad to worse the next week, when the Packers lost to the talent-starved Chicago Bears, 14-13, at Lambeau Field. Green Bay went into the game as a nine-point favorite but lost when Bears defensive end Bryan Robinson blocked Ryan Longwell's last-second, 28-yard field-goal attempt.

Almost incidentally, the game marked Favre's 117th consecutive start, breaking the record for consecutive starts by a quarterback previously held by Ron Jaworski. Later in the season, Favre reached 30,000 passing yards faster than all but two quarterbacks (Dan Marino and Warren Moon) in NFL history.

But the spiraling Packers would go on to lose six of their final 10 games and miss the playoffs for the first time in seven years. Favre threw for 4,091 yards, but had more interceptions (23) than touchdowns (22) and completed just 57.3% of his passes, the lowest mark of his career until he completed 56.0% in 2006.

On Jan. 2, 2000, just hours after the Packers beat the Arizona Cardinals in their regular-season finale but were officially eliminated from the playoffs by Dallas' victory over the New York Giants, Wolf summoned Rhodes to his office at Lambeau Field and fired the coach and his staff.

"I tell people all the time Ray was one of the best coaches I never had a chance to play for," Dotson said with a chuckle. "I think he was the head coach for about 340 days (actually 356)."

Despite the team's disappointing 8-8 record, Favre demonstrated the heart of a champion as he fought through debilitating pain and single-handedly carried the Packers to several victories. Perhaps Wolf said it best, after the season-

(above) Guard Marco Rivera and center Jeff Dellenbach help Favre after he was hit on a play in which the 49ers were called for unnecessary roughness in January 1999 in San Francisco. The 49ers won, 30-27, knocking the Packers out of the playoffs. (opposite) 49ers defensive end Chike Okeafor upends Favre in November 1999. Green Bay won, 20-3.

opening victory over Oakland at Lambeau Field:

"There's never been a player like this, and I don't care what anybody says, that's ever played on this field like him. Who's going to top him? We're talking about as rare a player to play in this era...as there is. I think the legend of Brett Favre continues to grow." ❹

CHANGING OF THE GUARD

Favre continues to thrive under new system

By Lori Nickel

Change was everywhere. Change at head coach. Change at general manager. Change in offensive philosophy.

A new Lambeau. A new millennium.

But no change at quarterback. No. 4 kept flinging underhanded passes, kept squirting around defensive ends, kept finding new targets downfield and making Pro Bowl players out of them. Kept workin' while everything and everyone around him kept changin'.

Brett Favre was in his early 30s, and while the retirement questions started popping up everywhere, the good years were not all behind him.

In 2000, the Packers got new coach Mike Sherman his first victory in the form of a 6-3 battle over Philadelphia. Sherman likened the experience to a visit with the dentist.

"Hey, I've had some pretty losses, where you just light it up, and you lose, and nothing felt good about that," Favre said at the time. He threw three interceptions and was sacked five times but came through on the final drive by completing 4 of 4 passes for 59 yards. "You can call it an ugly win, but it's a win."

The first three years of the Favre-Sherman era would mean lots of grinding victories and 10 fourth-quarter comebacks led by Favre, but by now, Favre was very set in his ways. That would test Sherman, who didn't like to roll the dice. He wanted sound football: few penalties, fewer dropped passes, next to no turnovers.

In 2000, Favre had only 20 passing touchdowns – the third-lowest in his career – but he also only threw a manageable total of 16 interceptions. Sherman hired Tom Rossley as offensive coordinator, who harped on the turnovers.

Rossley was also Favre's fifth quarterbacks coach, and his dry personality was nothing like former assistants Steve Mariucci, Marty Mornhinweg, Mike McCarthy or Andy Reid. Even-tempered and conservative, Rossley had ambitious plans for Favre that first summer in 2000. He wanted to cut down the turnovers, and he thought the best way to do that would be to work on Favre's mechanics, to correct his awkward footwork, to give him structure, cut down on the ad-lib plays.

In a 2005 interview, Favre grinned at the memory of Rossley's renovation project. He said he enjoyed working with Rossley as much as any of the other assistants he'd had, but the reining in part?

"Oh, I never bought into that," Favre said. "I tried. Sure. My whole career I've had to cut down on this or cut down on that. Mike Holmgren used to say this: We've got to be willing to accept one of those bad ones because of the five great ones we can get in return.

Favre leaps for joy as Mike McKenzie (not shown) returns an intercepted pass for a touchdown against Chicago in December 2003. The Packers won, 34-21, typical of the Favre era, when they were 22-10 against Chicago.

Tom Lynn

Jeffrey Phelps

(left) Classic form: Favre was fond of saying he would not advocate teaching his mechanics, especially his footwork, to anyone. But sometimes he did go by the book, such as when he fired this pass against Dallas in a 41-20 victory in October 2004. (above) Head coach Mike Sherman congratulates Favre after a touchdown drive against the Bears in January 2005 in Chicago. The Packers won, 31-14.

"I understand I can't turn the ball over and make costly mistakes, but I also know if I drop back 600 times, there's going to be times where it happens. As long as I make way more than my share of good ones, then I can deal with the bad ones, as ugly as they may be sometimes.

"I would never teach anyone my mechanics. I don't even know if they're teachable. So when Tom first came in, he wanted to work on my footwork. I thought it was a joke. I figured, hey, I'll give him a challenge.

"After two weeks he said, 'We'll work on something else.'"

Nothing changed about Favre on the field. He was still a hard-headed, tough player who wouldn't sit. Favre had to miss the final three exhibition games of the 2000 season with tendinitis in his throwing elbow. The elbow bothered him in the opening loss to the New York Jets in which he also sprained his thumb. But in Week 2, he completed his first 14 attempts and was 25 of 35 for 269 yards in a loss to

(left) Favre throws Tampa Bay safety Dexter Jackson out
of bounds after an interception in November 2002 in
Tampa. The Packers lost, 21-7. (above) Michael Strahan
of the New York Giants sacks Favre to set an NFL season
record of 22 ½ sacks Jan. 6, 2002, in East Rutherford, N.J.
Many people believe Favre intentionally gave up the
sack, but Favre denied that. The Packers won, 34-25.

Buffalo. Favre had no problem whipping up more of that
old comeback potion, either. There was the Philadelphia
game, then San Francisco, 31-28, Minnesota, 26-20 in
overtime, and Tampa Bay, 17-14, after being tied with each
team in the fourth quarter. Favre beat the Vikings on a 43-
yard rocket that bounced off Antonio Freeman's shoulder
before he raced into the end zone for the thrilling victory in
soaking wet conditions.

Those comebacks were exhilarating – for everyone else.
Looking back, Favre saw that the energy and effort it took
to win those games was exhausting. Each one took a little
more from the tank.

"You can't expect to win every game on the last play,"
Favre said in 2005. "There was a false sense of security
from our fans and the players. Maybe I was the only one to
realize how difficult that was because I was having to pull
the trigger. Having to win on the last play, it's great when
you win 'em. Man, was that exciting.

"But it takes its toll on you mentally. I joke about gray hair and all those things, but I think there is some truth to stress aging you quicker, and making you more numb, not only to bad times but to good times. Success sometimes doesn't mean what it used to. Nor does defeat, just because, I've seen it all. I always feel like I can be the difference-maker. But after a while, if you don't count on or rely on the other guys around you, I just know mentally it's taken its toll. Physically it is what it is, but mentally I think it's the biggest challenge an older player faces."

When Favre said this, the 2005 Packers were 1-6.

"I mean, I still love to play the game so much," Favre said. "I'm not getting comfortable with losing, but, to a certain degree, I've almost accepted it. I mean, I've come to the realization that there's only so much you can do. Had we lost those games in 2000, and we were 1-4 as opposed to 3-1 or whatever, I mean, it would have been very difficult, but yet, mentally, I think it would have been just as draining

Favre lies in pain after being tackled by Washington's LaVar Arrington in October 2002 in a 30-9 Green Bay victory. Despite injuring his knee, Favre played the next game.

as it was to win them."

Still, with Sherman as the leader, these were the years Favre would dump all his dome baggage on the carpet of the Metrodome. He could finally come away victorious there in 2000 with 290 yards and three touchdowns in an upset of the Vikings.

Yet the Packers finished with just one more victory than in 1999, at 9-7, and missed the playoffs. Uncertainly filled the air. Were the Packers rebounding? Or were they, slowly, receding from their great Super Bowl teams? Wasn't decline inevitable?

"When you've had so many ups and downs, and have been fortunate to play the game as long as I have, you've

David Joles

Jeffrey Phelps

Favre loses the ball late in the playoff game against Atlanta on Jan. 4, 2003, in Green Bay. Atlanta won, 27-7, dealing Green Bay its first playoff loss at Lambeau Field.

seen everything, you've dealt with everything," Favre said. "Which is good in a way, but it's bad in other ways because in some ways the luster is gone.

"A team that has won the Super Bowl probably is not quite as hungry as a team who hasn't won. I mean, that's hard to say for sure, but you can always hold your hat on, well, we won one. Or I've done this one, or I've done that, as opposed to, I haven't, so I'm a little more eager.

"Sometimes I think it's not even conscious, I think it's subconscious. You feel like, well, we've won a Super Bowl, so I'll give it my best, but if it doesn't work out, maybe that allows you to slide one way or another one day. I think for me that's how it's taken it's toll, is, I realize you're not going to win every one of them, and that is disappointing."

Help would be on the way in two forms for Favre. Big-time.

A formidable offensive line of left tackle Chad Clifton, left guard Mike Wahle, center Mike Flanagan, right guard Marco Rivera and right tackle Mark Tauscher had played together enough in 2000 to become a solid and complete unit in 2001. Even when injuries hit this line, and certainly when it was healthy, it meant everything for Favre. They

Tom Lynn

(left) A hungry Brett Favre chomps down on a turkey leg as he and Ahman Green share player of the game honors after beating the Lions 29-27 on Thanksgiving Day 2001 at the Silverdome. (above) Favre tosses his chin strap after throwing an interception at Philadelphia in a 19-14 loss in Philadelphia in 2005. Favre's longevity enabled him to set the NFL record for career touchdown passes with 442, and also led to him holding the mark for career interceptions at 288.

Jeffrey Phelps

protected him from sacks and pressures, which not only allowed him to throw in the pocket, it meant he didn't take the beating he could have in his early 20s.

In 2001, Favre became the first player in NFL history to have 10 consecutive 3,000-yard passing seasons. Packers receiver Donald Driver believes that offensive line was the best in the NFL at the time.

"He was more relaxed playing behind them," Driver said in 2005. "When he's relaxed in the pocket and he doesn't have that type of pressure on him, he's dangerous. I think everyone in the National Football League knows that. If you give him time to sit in the pocket, he'll kill you."

The Packers finished 12-4 in 2001. They beat San Francisco at home in the playoffs but then went on to a dis-

Favre shows his joy after a 25-15 victory over San Francisco in a wild-card playoff game Jan. 13, 2002. But the next week, Favre threw six interceptions in a 45-17 loss to the Rams.

astrous showing at St. Louis, losing, 45-17. Favre was intercepted six times.

In 2002, Sherman perhaps did his best all-around coaching. The Packers were besieged by injuries, but thanks to strong contributions from the rookie class, the Packers again compiled a 12-4 record.

In his 12th season, Favre led the NFC with 27 touchdown passes, and he got some consideration for the MVP award. Favre became just the third quarterback to throw for more

than 300 career touchdowns that year.

But for the first time for any Packer, Green Bay lost a playoff game at home. Michael Vick and the Atlanta Falcons upset the Packers, 27-7.

This was hard on everyone, especially Favre, who at the time was still consistently bringing up Super Bowl goals.

"Now I definitely realize that I'm human and this organization is human," Favre said in 2005.

Through these middle years of Favre's career, his world kept changing. After a close vote, taxpayers agreed to a $295 million renovation of Lambeau Field. The Packers got a better locker room and excellent meeting room facilities in the remodeling.

In March 2001, Favre had three years left on his existing contract, but he and the Packers agreed to a 10-year extension that would all but guarantee he would play the rest of his career in Green Bay. The deal was for $101.5 million, making him the highest-paid player in the NFL.

It was the last move outgoing general manager Ron Wolf oversaw before handing all of the controls over to Sherman.

Wolf announced his retirement in February 2001, then worked through the draft. While Favre would forever feel grateful to coach Mike Holmgren, he also would never forget it was Wolf who first believed in him. In Wolf, Favre found almost unconditional faith in his abilities. The two remain close to this day.

"When he left I said, 'There's another piece of the puzzle leaving.' It was more of a wake-up call to me. As I look around now, I am the last man here," Favre said in 2005. "In a way I think that's a pat on my back, to still be here, but I hated losing him, losing Mike Holmgren, losing Steve Mariucci. Ron and I became real close because we were like the only ones left. And I proved him right. For him to give me that opportunity I was never going to prove him wrong." ❹

Favre shares a moment with general manager Ron Wolf during practice in Green Bay in March 2001. Favre spoke of his appreciation for Wolf's unwavering faith in the quarterback's abilities.

LONG SEASONS OF HEARTACHES

Series of personal tragedies turns Favre's world upside down

By Lori Nickel

"Good timber does not grow with ease; the stronger the wind, the stronger the trees."— J. Willard Marriott

How much can one man handle?

A broken thumb? For Green Bay Packers quarterback Brett Favre, sure, it was rough, but of course he'd play through it.

But the sudden death of his father? Well, that hurt like nothing else.

Then Favre found out tragic news about his young brother-in-law, and then his wife had cancer. Cancer. The word alone sent chills through him.

Then former teammate Reggie White died unexpectedly, and surely, this couldn't all be happening in a 14-month span. How long can one man hold it together when everything else seems to be falling apart?

From October 2003 to the end of the 2004 season, Favre endured one form of personal adversity after another. Football, which had been his whole world, became a respite. At least on the field, Favre might have some control of what happened.

The 2003 Green Bay Packers season started with a disappointing loss to Minnesota in the official unveiling of the newly renovated Lambeau Field. Then the Packers took a 3-3 record into Week 7, and that's when the tone of the season changed.

On Oct. 19, Favre broke the thumb on his right, throwing hand at St. Louis after he slammed it into the shoulder pad of lineman Mike Wahle. Favre shook off the injury and kept playing. He would spend nine weeks on the NFL injury report, the second-most in his career.

He wore a splint that both preserved his record-setting consecutive starting streak at quarterback and drove him absolutely nuts. The injured thumb

(left) Favre leaves the field in Oakland with his wife, Deanna, after playing what he called the best game of his career Dec. 22, 2003, one day after learning his father had died. The Packers defeated the Raiders, 41-7, in a game that served as Favre's stirring tribute to beloved dad, Irvin, who had coached him in high school. Millions in the Monday Night Football television audience shared the emotional night with the grief-stricken Favre family.
(above) Favre waves to his wife in a luxury box after his fourth touchdown pass of the game in Oakland.

Tom Lynn

Jeffrey Phelps

(opposite) Favre throws a touchdown pass to Wesley Walls while being pressured by the Raiders' Lorenzo Bromell during the first quarter Dec. 22, 2003. Favre played despite learning of the death of his father the day before. (above) Favre examines his thumb before taking the field for a game the Packers lost, 17-14, to Philadelphia in November 2003. Despite the injury, iron man Favre led the Packers to the playoffs. He threw an NFL-best 32 touchdown passes – 19 of them after he broke the thumb – and made the Pro Bowl.

helped contribute to fumbles and poor play for a few weeks, but Favre was still the leader of the Packers in victories against Minnesota in a rematch, Chicago and San Diego.

Still, the Packers were struggling to make the playoffs, sitting at 8-6 and trailing Minnesota in the divisional standings. Green Bay had to get a victory at Oakland on "Monday Night Football."

The day before the game, Favre learned that his father, Irvin, died of a heart attack while driving his car in

"That night solidified everything I already knew about Brett Favre."

Antonio Freeman,
Packers wide receiver, on the night when Favre led the team to victory one day after his dad had died

Mississippi. "Big Irv" was Brett's high school coach, his mentor and one of the closest people to him.

"I remember that day. I remember the uncertainty," Antonio Freeman said in 2005. He was a Packers receiver from 1995-2001 and again in 2003. "Brett came to our team meeting that night – his whole face was just pink.

"He had probably been crying, he was probably holding in a lot of tears. When you lose someone of that magnitude, you use your family to console you. He had no true family. Yeah, he had the team, but Deanna wasn't there, the kids weren't there, he wasn't in the comfort of his own home.

"I think of all the things he had to deal with. He couldn't go anywhere, and he had to deal with getting that news, of having to make a sudden decision about – do you play or do you not, not having your family with you, being confined – all those things running together in about a three-hour period. It could have been very easy for him to walk away from that football team and say, 'Well, this is too much. This is my best friend, my dad, this is my everything, and it's too much for me,' and we all would have respected that.

"He handled it like a true champ. He handled it like the true competitor that he is. He said that his dad would have wanted him to play. It was a magical night. I still think back to that night and it was unbelievable. That night solidified everything I already knew about Brett Favre."

Favre played what he called the best game of his entire career – MVP seasons, Super Bowls included.

Favre threw for 399 yards, four touchdowns and had a team-record passer rating of 154.9, just three points from perfect. The Packers rolled over the Raiders, 41-7.

The Packers flew Deanna out for the game, and the two walked off the field together, a moment that became one of the most memorable photos of Favre's career. That

game was the best way Favre – at first nervous and then emotional – could pay tribute to the man he both admired and tried to please every time he put on a football jersey.

"I was afraid I wouldn't play well," Favre said in 2005. "That day of the game, I'd almost forgotten who we were playing. I forgot all the stuff I prepared for all week. Here I am on the national stage, which is tough anyway, we're in a situation where we need to win, and all of a sudden, I couldn't tell you what they do on defense. I went blank.

"Playing is one thing. Going out there and honoring your father is another."

Around that time, Favre also made the Pro Bowl, despite the thumb injury, because he helped lead the Packers to 442 points, the second-highest in team history. He also threw an NFL-best 32 touchdown passes – 19 of them after that St. Louis game in which he broke the thumb.

The Packers won their last four games of the season, finished 10-6 and benefited from a total collapse by Minnesota. Arizona's Nate Poole caught a last-second, deep fourth-down pass to beat Minnesota, 18-17. The Packers claimed the NFC North Division title and headed to the playoffs red-hot.

Favre mourned the loss of his father in front of everyone and wondered if destiny had a role in the latest events.

"Something's going on here," Favre said at the time.

In the playoffs, the Packers won a thrilling home game against Seattle in overtime on an interception return for a touchdown by Al Harris. But the team of destiny met its fate. In the second round, the Packers would not be able to hold Philadelphia on a fourth-and-26 play on defense.

The Eagles also threw a blitz that tripped up Favre just enough to force him to throw a late, game-changing interception. Eagles coach Andy Reid, Favre's former quarterbacks coach in Green Bay, said he was just trying to make

(left) Favre stretches in vain for a first down while being tackled by Philadelphia Eagles safety Michael Lewis during the fourth quarter of a playoff game in January 2004 in Philadelphia. The Packers' season ended that day after they could not hold the Eagles on a fourth-and-26 play. Green Bay everntually lost the game in overtime, 20-17.

a play and swore he didn't have the kryptonite only someone that close to Favre would know about.

"No, I mean, he's seen everything," Reid said in 2005. "We happened to catch it right. We needed to make a play at that time or we weren't going to be in that ball game."

The Packers had their eyes on an NFC Championship Game with Carolina, and maybe a good shot at the Super Bowl. But in an instant, the season was over. Favre went home for a quiet off-season during which he was seldom heard from publicly.

The 2004 season began with a 1-4 start and a humiliating Monday night showing against Tennessee at Lambeau.

Soon after, in October 2004, Deanna Favre's brother, Casey Tynes, died in an all-terrain vehicle accident on the Favre property in Mississippi.

Still coming to terms with her brother's death, and admittedly numb, Deanna then learned a lump in her breast was cancer. Though she caught it early and was given an excel-

Favre and tackle Brad Bedell lie on the turf after Favre threw an interception against Minnesota on Jan. 9, 2005, at Lambeau Field. The Vikings eliminated the Packers from the playoffs, 31-17. The loss occurred two weeks after Favre endured yet another tragedy, the death of former teammate Reggie White at age 43.

lent prognosis for recovery, she would need months of treatment – a lumpectomy, chemotherapy and radiation, all of which left her tired and at times very down.

"Cancer, it is as close to death as you can get," Brett Favre said. "As soon as I heard cancer, I thought, this is not good. When she told me that, my reaction was, you have got to be kidding me. I didn't feel sorry for myself, I felt sorry for her because she's always been the one who's kind of carried the load.

"I can't say that I ever asked, why me or why us. It was, 'How much more?' "

Favre (center) is among the pallbearers at the funeral for former Packer Reggie White on Dec. 30, 2004, at the United Park Baptist Church in Charlotte, N.C. Other pallbearers were Wayne Dozier, Michael Perry, Adrian Murrell, Christopher Tillison, Eugene Robinson, Hardy Nickerson and Shawn White.

Two days after the Packers clinched their third consecutive NFC North Division championship with a 34-31 victory at Minnesota on Christmas Eve, in which Favre orchestrated 80-yard and 76-yard drives to win the game in the fourth quarter, White died. One of the NFL's greatest defensive linemen was only 43. He was very close to Favre as one of the leaders of the 1996 Super Bowl championship team. Favre missed a practice to be a pallbearer at White's funeral.

Through it all, Favre's numbers for 2004 were undeniably remarkable. He was still at the top of his game. He passed for 4,088 yards, 30 touchdowns and a 92.4 passer rating. Behind a solid offense that carried the team, Green Bay finished strong late in the season and made the playoffs.

But there they were, simply stung by Minnesota in the first round at Lambeau Field. Favre was sacked, threw interceptions and the Packers in general were mistake-prone. It was such a horrible game that Favre would have called it a career right then and there if he had been impulsive.

He didn't. He waited and gave himself time instead of making a rushed, and maybe regrettable, decision. He waited for Deanna's strength to return and for life that was cancer-free.

Deanna has since thrown herself into an advocacy role for breast cancer patients, starting her own Deanna Favre Hope Foundation. She helps raise money to pay for treatments for women in financial need.

When she was OK, Favre really started to miss the game and knew he had at least another season in him. He had hoped the personal turmoil was behind him.

"The thing about Brett is, even in the toughest of times, he was going to have fun doing what he did, and he was passionate about it," Reid said. "His overall toughness. You weren't going to keep him off the football field. Those are two things you really respect in him."

About two months after the end of the 2004 season, Favre said he'd come back for a 14th season in Green Bay in 2005. He'd come back a changed man in one way.

"One time in my life, for a long period of my life, football was all that really mattered," Favre said. "Everything else just kind of followed along with it. I lost Dad, and Dad was so much a part of my football career, just as much as life in general. Most of the time we talked, it was football. It wasn't, 'Hey, how's life going,' it was football. So when I lost him, it took a big chunk of football away from me.

"Then to lose Deanna's brother and have her face cancer, which is a family crisis, just made football seem so secondary. I would not want to have anyone go through what I went through to realize there is more to life than football.

"But it kind of opened my eyes to, this is a small period in your life; there are a lot of things much more important than football." ❹

Jeffrey Phelps

AN EXCLUSIVE FRATERNITY

Quarterback looks back fondly at his hundreds of teammates

By Gary D'Amato

Sometimes, after one of those frenzied fourth-quarter comebacks, or after he eluded a six-man rush by spinning and stumbling and slipping and scrambling – and then heaved an off-the-back-foot, across-the-field, game-winning touchdown pass – the announcers would gasp and chuckle and say something like this:

"Brett Favre single-handedly won this game for the Green Bay Packers."

OK, technically that's true. Favre throws the ball with his right hand (though he was known, when wearing a 300-pound defensive tackle on his shoulder pads, to flip it back-handed with his left).

But single-handedly, as in all by himself?

Well, a receiver had to catch the ball. Somebody had to

> *"He changed the way I approached the game. He played every game like it was his last, and he practiced that way. I tried to model myself after Reggie."*
>
> **Brett Favre,**
> on his late teammate Reggie White

block. A running back had to execute a play-action fake or pick up a blitzing linebacker in the hole. The coaches had to draw up the play and teach it in practice. And the defense had to keep the game close enough to make a comeback possible.

Favre always subscribed to the theory that the quarterback gets too much credit in victory and too much blame in defeat. Fair or not, it goes with the territory. Stand under center and you're the center of attention. You're the guy with the bull's-eye on your back and the game's outcome, on occasion, in the palm of your hand.

Favre's record over 17 National Football League seasons is unimpeachable. He is a first-ballot lock for the Hall of Fame, his record for consecutive starts by a quarterback may never be broken and he holds virtually every league passing record.

But he would be the first to admit he had a lot of help along the way.

Since 1992, when Favre arrived in Green Bay, 415 players have suited up for at least one regular-season or playoff game with the Packers, according to team records.

More than 30 of those players can brag to their grand-

After general manager Ron Wolf acquired Reggie White, the respect White and Favre had for each other helped them resurrect a winning tradition in Green Bay, ending decades filled mostly with futility.

children that they appeared in exactly one NFL game with Favre, who would be excused if he barely remembered some of them. The names Jeff Blackshear, Tunch Ilkin, Terdell Sands, Moe Smith and David Viaene don't exactly resonate in Packers lore.

On the other end of the spectrum, fullback William Henderson played in 188 games with Favre and long snapper Rob Davis played in 167. Others appearing in at least 100 games with Favre were: LeRoy Butler, Gilbert Brown, Chad Clifton, Earl Dotson, Donald Driver, Bubba Franks, Antonio Freeman, Kabeer Gbaja-Biamila, Bernardo Harris, George Koonce, Dorsey Levens, Ryan Longwell, Marco Rivera, Darren Sharper, Mark Tauscher, Tyrone Williams and Frank Winters.

Furthermore, during Favre's 16 seasons in Green Bay, 24 teammates were selected to play in the Pro Bowl.

"There's just so many guys who have meant a lot to my career," Favre said in 2005.

But which player or players influenced him the most? In no particular order, he ticks off the names Sterling Sharpe, Reggie White and Butler.

Sharpe didn't even play three full seasons with Favre before suffering a career-ending neck injury in 1994 but left an indelible impression on the young quarterback by catching 108 passes in 1992 and 112 in '93.

"He was the most talented wide receiver I've played with," Favre said. "If he wouldn't have gotten hurt I don't know if I would have developed as fast because I relied on him more than I did on my talent. There would be three guys on him and I'd throw it to him and he'd catch it. After he got hurt, I had to throw to different guys.

"Sterling liked to run his mouth, but I'll tell you what, he

(right) Receiver Donald Driver picks up Favre after being taken out late in a 26-7 victory over Chicago in December 2006. Driver became one of Favre's closest friends on the team in addition to a favorite target. (opposite) Favre gathers his offensive linemen for a moment on the field after that season-ending victory over the Bears. Many thought Favre wanted the photo as a remembrance of his last game, but they were like a cornerback biting on a pump fake: Favre returned to play a magnificent final season in 2007.

was pretty damned good. He never practiced but he caught 100 balls two years in a row, which is phenomenal."

Then there was the late White, the larger-than-life defensive end who arrived in Green Bay via free agency in 1993. Together, White and Favre led the Packers to a 66-30 record over the next six seasons, including a victory in Super Bowl XXXI.

Favre said no other teammate, before or since, made a bigger impression than White in terms of combining talent and leadership on the field and integrity and decency off it.

"Greatest player I've ever been around," Favre said.

"Even though I was a quarterback by position, I was a lineman deep inside. I related to those guys."

Brett Favre

"Greatest teammate. Greatest person. Game-changer. Game-breaker. What more can you say?

"He changed the way I approached the game. He played every game like it was his last, and he practiced that way. I tried to model myself after Reggie. When needed, he could make those big plays and in practice he was a phenomenal leader. He was rare. Guys like him don't come along too

Jeffrey Phelps

often. On top of all that, you couldn't block him."

Asked to name one former teammate he'd like to have back on the roster, Favre picked Butler, the safety who played in 181 games from 1990-2001. Butler was the Packers' yin to Favre's yang, a respected and well-liked player who backed up his playful chatter with big plays on the field.

"He was a great player and a great teammate, and no one had as much fun as LeRoy," Favre said. "I think I've taken a lot from all the guys I've played with, and having fun like LeRoy did is important because it can be a grind. Even when you're winning it can be a grind.

"LeRoy always made it competitive in practice. When we ran our goal-line or 2-minute offense I really wanted to beat him because I knew he was going to rub it in if I didn't. That made me a better player."

Then there are his targets. Favre has thrown touchdown passes to 44 players, from Kitrick Taylor, who caught the

The "Three Amigos": Mark Chmura, Favre and Frank Winters were teammates and close friends. Here they pose in New Orleans at Super Bowl XXXI media day.

game-winner against the Cincinnati Bengals on Sept. 20, 1992 – the pass that launched the Brett Favre era – to rookie James Jones in 2008.

Freeman caught 57 touchdown passes from Favre and made the catch the quarterback calls the single greatest play he has ever seen: a description-defying, 43-yard game-winner on Nov. 6, 2000, in overtime against the Minnesota Vikings in a Monday night game at rain-soaked Lambeau Field.

Favre lobbed the ball toward the right sideline, where Freeman was being covered by Vikings cornerback Chris Dishman, who tipped the pass off his right hand and then his left arm. Freeman, sliding on the muddy turf,

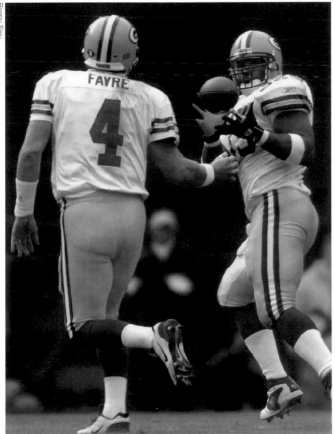

somehow caught the ball after it first bounced off his shoulder and face mask.

With the Vikings defenders and almost everyone else in the stadium thinking the play was over, Freeman alertly jumped to his feet and ran to the end zone.

"I tell people all the time I'd like to take credit for that play," Favre said. "The best thing I did was throw an awful ball and allow Antonio to do what he did best, which was make a play.

"I think not just in Packers history, but in NFL history it will go down as one of the greatest catches ever. It wasn't the Super Bowl, but it was a Monday night game, overtime. Just a phenomenal catch."

Over the years, Favre has handed off to some exceptional running backs, too. Edgar Bennett gained 1,000 yards in 1995, Levens did it twice in a three-year span (1997, '99) and Ahman Green did it five consecutive seasons (2000-'04) before an injury ended his streak in 2005.

Green set the Packers' single-season record with 1,883 yards in 2003.

"Dorsey was maybe the best all-around back I've played with," Favre said. "He didn't do everything great but he did everything good. Some backs run good routes but they don't have good hands. He was the total package.

"Ahman is the greatest pure runner I've played with. He probably changed my role a little bit because we've run it so good with him."

We'll never know if one or more of Favre's backups over the years would have had success as the Packers' starting quarterback, but several of them have gone on to productive careers as starters with other teams, including Mark Brunell, Aaron Brooks and Matt Hasselbeck.

Favre said the fact he had quality backups for most of

(above) Backup quarterback Matt Hasselbeck and Favre confer during a game at Buffalo in September 2000. Hasselbeck, like some other Favre understudies, went on to a successful career as a starter. In Hasselbeck's case, it was in Seattle under former Packers coach Mike Holmgren. (left) Favre gets off an 8-yard pass to fullback William Henderson in San Diego in December 2003. Henderson was a key blocker and outlet receiver for Favre throughout much of his career.

Rick Wood

his career was one factor in his streak of 253 consecutive starts. He admitted there were times he probably should have sat out a game or two but feared losing his job.

"I always remembered I got my job because Don (Majkowski) got hurt," he said. "I never forgot that. You're only a play away from either playing or not playing. So many guys who lost their jobs figured, 'I'll be right back in there when I'm healthy' and they never played again.

"I didn't want to give someone else a chance."

Though Favre played with some brilliant play-makers on both sides of the ball, his closest friends generally were linemen, and that dates to his days at Southern Mississippi, where his roommate all four years was offensive tackle Chris Ryals.

Favre always gravitated to the guys who duke it out in the trenches, and not just because they protected his backside. There's something about a lineman's toughness, loyalty and perpetually dirty uniform that appealed to him.

For several years in the 1990s, tight end Mark Chmura, Winters and Favre were practically joined at the hip.

"It's probably more my mentality or makeup," he said. "Even though I was a quarterback by position, I was a lineman deep inside. I related to those guys.

"People have looked at the quarterback as the pansy and the linemen as the tough guys. I was never a pretty boy, never a prima donna. I wanted to play the position like a lineman, play it tough and be accountable and durable and reliable."

All of Favre's teammates from the early years in Green Bay have retired. Some of them, such as Bennett and James Campen, are coaches now. Other longtime teammates, such as Mike Wahle, Rivera and Green, departed as free agents.

As the Packers' roster continued to turn over, Favre remained the constant, until his retirement in March 2008. ❹

Freestyle Freeman: In one of the most spectacular plays of the Favre era, Minnesota cornerback Cris Dishman drops a potential interception and the ball bounces off the left arm of Green Bay wide receiver Antonio Freeman, who had slipped and was on the ground. Freeman controlled the ball against his chest as he lay on the ground. He jumped to his feet at the 15, eluded safety Robert Griffith and scored the touchdown that gave the Packers a 26-20 victory in overtime at Lambeau Field on Nov. 6, 2000.

Mark Hoffman

SMASHING SUCCESS

Favre's ability to avoid injury was a factor in record-setting career

By Lori Nickel

It was perhaps fitting that Brett Favre would rewrite the National Football League passing record book in Green Bay, where, more than 80 years ago, Packers founder Curly Lambeau was the first coach in the league to regularly use the forward pass.

After 16 years with the Packers, Favre completed his 17-year career as the NFL's all-time leader in touchdown passes (442), completions (5,377), attempts (8,758), yards (61,555) and victories (160).

Of all the statistics, however, it's Favre's starting streak that tops the list. He did not miss a start after taking over Sept. 27, 1992, against Pittsburgh. Through injured thumbs, shredded ankles, pain-killer addiction, the death of his father and an array of other injuries and hardships, he was the starting quarterback for the Packers.

He started 253 straight regular-season games, 275 including playoffs, the NFL record for quarterbacks and the second-longest recorded streak in league history. The streak ended only when Favre announced his retirement in March 2008.

"Brett's streak is very impressive just given the nature of how demanding the quarterback position is," Indianapolis Colts quarterback Peyton Manning said in 2005. "To be able to answer the starting bell for so many seasons is one of the great accomplishments in sports, and it means a great deal to everyone connected with the organization."

At the end of the 2007 season, Manning stood second behind Favre with 160 consecutive starts over 10 years. Ron Jaworski is third at 116.

"That (streak) is something that is actually very incredible," Dan Marino, the former Miami quarterback who is now an NFL analyst for CBS, said in 2005. "I had a couple of streaks going for a while. I went for 145 in a row and 95 in a row and it is mind-boggling to think the game being so physical and the style that Brett plays, that he has not missed a game. It is pretty special.

"If there is a guy who may get a chance to come close it is Peyton Manning. He is a durable guy and like Brett Favre he knows what to do with the football. He is not taking too many big hits and he doesn't hold the ball. He gets rid of it like Brett."

Indeed, the streak is Favre's greatest source of satisfaction because he wanted to be the one everyone could rely on.

"That's an amazing statistic to me," Favre said in 2005, "because it means that you've played at a high enough level. Physically, it's tough, it's demanding, but I've played

After breaking the NFL record for career touchdown passes, Favre hoists its recipient, Greg Jennings, in a 23-16 victory over the Vikings on Sept. 30, 2007, in Minneapolis. Favre's 421st touchdown pass eclipsed Dan Marino's record.

well enough on a consistent basis that they say, 'We're not worried about that position. If he has an off game, it's one of a handful over 200-something.' That is something I'm the most proud of."

But the other records are a symbol of Favre's endurance as well. When he was pursuing Marino's record 420 touchdown passes, he knew achieving the feat would give him a lasting place in history.

"Four-hundred-twenty touchdown passes, it would be kind of cool, because 20 years from now, a lot of people won't remember me playing," Favre said. "Kind of like I don't remember Johnny Unitas. If it wasn't for stuff in print, or NFL films, he would be forgotten. So I could say 20 years from now, 'Hey, look at the record books, I got the most touchdown passes.'"

While he didn't like watching his records fall, Marino admired Favre's career.

"You can tell that he has passion and love for the competition," Marino said. "And I have always felt that to be a great quarterback you have to love the competition and the game. You love the wins, but the losses hurt more, and for great players they hurt more than anybody else on the team. And Brett seems to be that kind of guy."

Favre remains among the leaders in several other NFL categories, but a few do stand out.

Only two players have ever won back-to-back NFL Most Valuable Player awards: Joe Montana (1989-'90) and Manning (2004, co-MVP with Steve McNair in 2003).

Only Favre has won it three times in a row: in 1995, 1996 and as co-MVP with Barry Sanders in 1997.

"It meant a lot to him and our team when he won that third MVP award," said Andy Reid, Favre's quarterbacks coach in Green Bay and now the coach of Philadelphia.

Favre, a certain Hall of Famer, greets another future Hall of Famer, Miami's Dan Marino, before their exhibition game in September 1999 in Green Bay.

"He made the whole team feel a part of that. Everybody took so much pride in that. He made it very clear that you don't do it alone; you do it with a strong offensive line, tough receivers, running backs doing their jobs, the opportunity with getting the ball back from the defense. He tied it into everybody, and everybody was pulling for

120

After throwing another interception, Favre lies on the ground with his hand bloodied in a 27-7 loss to Seattle in 1999 in Green Bay.

him to get it. That was unique."

As long as it will be remembered that Favre's first pass was actually to himself (off a deflection), his last pass will also forever be remembered as a costly interception. Favre was picked off in the 2007 season NFC Championship Game against the New York Giants at Lambeau Field, and the play led to the Giants' stunning upset in overtime.

Favre's reputation as a gambler goes hand in hand with his 288 career interceptions, also the NFL record. He surpassed George Blanda (277), John Hadl (268) and Fran Tarkenton (266).

The 80-year-old Blanda spent 26 years playing for the Chicago Bears, Baltimore Colts, Houston Oilers and Oakland Raiders and sincerely defended the gambling play that was Favre's trademark. And why shouldn't he? If there's anyone on the planet who understands what Favre was trying to do when he made so many of those interceptions, it is Blanda.

"Some people, when they're down two touchdowns and there's five minutes to play, they just keep throwing those short passes out in the flat," Blanda said. "And they move the ball down the field and they don't score! So all you do is run the time off the clock and your numbers look good.

"And then there are other quarterbacks like Brett and mys... well, I am not going to compare myself with him. But... the only way you can win is to try to make a big play. So you try to make 'em. If you don't make 'em, you're going to lose anyways. So you might as well try them."

Added Marino: "Interceptions are going to happen, especially if you are the type of player like Brett that takes chances. I was the same type player. There are times in games that you feel that you can make throws that other guys can't make, and you sometimes take those chances. Brett Favre has been an incredible player and there is no way that the interceptions that he has thrown take away from his career accomplishments."

Favre also has thrown a 99-yard touchdown pass to Robert Brooks, the longest in NFL history (tied with many others).

(left) Antonio Freeman catches the ball in front of New England defender Lawyer Milloy on his way to an 81-yard touchdown during Super Bowl XXXI on Jan. 26, 1997, in New Orleans. (above) After breaking the record for consecutive starts for a quarterback, Favre meets with the previous record-holder, former Philadelphia Eagle Ron Jaworski, during a 14-13 loss to the Bears on Nov. 7, 1999, in Green Bay.

When Favre walked away, he had led the Packers to 11 post-seasons, seven division crowns, four NFC Championship Games, two Super Bowls and a championship with a victory in Super Bowl XXXI.

Every year he wore No. 4 in Green Bay, he had at least 300 completions and 3,000 yards passing, both records, and 209 touchdowns at Lambeau Field, the most in a single stadium. In connecting on 66.5% of his passes in his final year – a personal best – he moved ahead of Marino with a 61.4 career completion percentage, making him the NFL's most accurate passer among those with at least 6,000 attempts.

With 63 games with three or more touchdown passes, Favre also placed just ahead of Marino (62) on the NFL's all-time list.

Of course, Favre is entrenched in the Green Bay annals with numerous records. His top target was Antonio Freeman, who caught more touchdown passes from Favre – 57 – than anyone else. Freeman said those numbers don't nearly define Favre's impact on the franchise.

"He's a Hall of Famer," Freeman said in 2005. "Those records, they come and go, there will be someone younger, someone faster, someone bigger, and they will shatter those records. But the memories, no one can ever take those. The journey was great. I could name 20 fantastic moments with him and I would still miss five that I should have included. That's how great the journey was. There was never a dull moment with him."

Favre has said his records don't define his great career.

"I think what I achieved here speaks for itself," Favre said. "To have to have something in print, to show someone, I guess it would be nice, but I think I've already proved my worth." ❹

(left) Donald Driver can only chase the Giants' Corey Webster after he intercepted a Favre pass in overtime of their NFC Championship Game on Jan. 20, 2008, in Green Bay. The pass was Favre's last in the NFL.

Jeffrey Phelps

FADING GLORY
Playoff struggles begin in late '90s
By Tom Silverstein

By the time he was 28 years old, Brett Favre stood alongside the likes of National Football League legends Joe Montana, Terry Bradshaw, Troy Aikman, Dan Marino and Bart Starr in post-season annals.

Just six years into his career as a starter, Favre ranked as one of only seven quarterbacks to throw for 3,000 yards in the playoffs and trailed only Montana, Marino, Bradshaw and Elway in career post-season touchdown passes with 25. His passer rating of 92.0 ranked fourth all-time behind Starr, Montana and Ken Anderson.

Having played in consecutive Super Bowls during the 1996 and '97 seasons, Favre was at the zenith of his playoff career.

Little could he, or anyone else, have known how cruel the post-season would be to him from that point on. As the Packers faded from their Super Bowl luminance, so did Favre's glorious playoff numbers.

Starting with the Packers' elimination in the first round of the playoffs on Terrell Owens' miracle catch on Jan. 3, 1999, to the infamous "fourth-and-26" loss against Philadelphia on Jan. 11, 2004, to the final pass of his career in 2008 – an overtime interception against the New York Giants – the playoffs were nothing but heartbreak and frustration for the three-time MVP.

"I was a rookie when we lost the Super Bowl to Denver," former Packers kicker Ryan Longwell said of the 1997 season. "All the superstars we had, I thought we'd go on forever. That San Francisco playoff game that next year, obviously we got a bum call with that Jerry Rice fumble, but after we lost that game it was kind of an eye-opener that it's not guaranteed that you're going to go to the Super Bowl every year.

"I think being a rookie I certainly took it for granted."

For Favre, it was a series of moments worth forgetting.

None was worse than Corey Webster's overtime interception in the NFC Championship Game on Jan. 20, 2008. In the frigid cold, with the wind chill reaching 24 degrees below zero, Favre under-threw receiver Donald Driver on an out route on the second play from scrimmage in overtime. The ball floated, and Webster cut in front of Driver for the interception, giving the Giants a first down at the Packers' 34 yard line.

Three plays later, Lawrence Tynes drilled a 47-yard field goal that gave the Giants a 23-20 victory and a trip to Super Bowl XLII.

For Favre, it would be the last game of his storied career. On the morning of March 4, 2008, word of his retirement hit the news. He ended his career 3-7 in his last 10 post-season games, including a loss to the Broncos in Super Bowl XXXII.

"As I look back on my career, no regrets," Favre said at his retirement news conference March 6, 2008. "No regrets, whatsoever. Sure, I would have liked to have won

Rams linebacker Tommy Polley scores a touchdown while Favre chases in vain during a playoff game Jan. 20, 2002, in St. Louis. The Rams won, 45-17, as Favre threw six interceptions, including three that were returned for touchdowns.

Jeffrey Phelps

Rick Wood

(opposite) Favre tries to get a pass off to Ahman Green while in the grasp of the Rams' Sean Moran during the 45-17 playoff loss to St. Louis on Jan. 20, 2002. The play was ruled a sack. (above) Favre and Atlanta quarterback Michael Vick meet on the field after their game Jan. 4, 2003. The Falcons won the playoff game, 27-7, the Packers' first playoff loss at home.

"I played the game one way, the only way I knew how."

Brett Favre

Championship Game with the Eagles debacle, and in '04 Favre threw four interceptions in another home playoff loss, this time to division rival Minnesota.

Except for '07, the Packers were never really on the brink of playing in a Super Bowl, and their playoff elimination in recent years was far from a fluke. Even in '98, coach Mike Holmgren's final season in Green Bay when the Packers still had the remnants of a Super Bowl team, the road to the Super Bowl would have run through the 15-1 Vikings, and the Packers would have been hard-pressed to make it for a third year in a row.

Despite 12-4 records in '01 and '02 and a 10-6 record in '04, the Packers were simply not Super Bowl caliber.

"In looking back there's no doubt the year we lost to Denver and I think the year following that season, which was Holmgren's last season, no one would argue that we were not as good as we were the previous year," Favre said in 2005. "And then I think with each year we probably could have said that.

"Records sometimes don't indicate how good you are either way. We gave ourselves some opportunities by getting in the playoffs, but we never capitalized on them."

After the Super Bowl loss to the Broncos, Favre had a 9-4 post-season record, and he had thrown for 3,098 yards and 23 touchdowns with 10 interceptions in those games. His passer rating of 92.0 was 2.7 points higher than his career regular-season rating.

Ten years later, his post-season record had fallen to 12-10 and his passer rating had dropped to 85.3. He had thrown 16 touchdown passes and 18 interceptions in going 3-6 since the loss to the Broncos.

Ten of those interceptions came in the losses to St. Louis and Minnesota, and they are one of the indelible marks left on Favre's playoff record in his later years.

"I take as much responsibility for the lack of production and the fact we didn't win in those games, just as much as

more games, would have liked to have gone to a Super Bowl this year, would have liked to have thrown less interceptions, more touchdowns, but no regrets."

It looked like 2007 would be the year Favre got back to the Super Bowl. Under second-year coach Mike McCarthy, he led the team to a 13-3 record and played superbly in a 42-20 divisional-round playoff victory over the Seattle Seahawks, played in a snowstorm at Lambeau Field.

But the year ended the way so many others had – in loss.

After missing out on the playoffs in '99 and 2000, the Packers came back in '01 under Mike Sherman only to bow out in the second round in a 45-17 loss to St. Louis in which Favre threw a playoff record-tying six interceptions, three of which were returned for touchdowns.

The following year the Packers suffered the first home playoff loss in franchise history to the Atlanta Falcons. In '03, the Packers blew a shot to play in the NFC

Jeffrey Phelps

(opposite) Packers defensive back Darren Sharper can only watch after his hit didn't stop the 49ers' Terrell Owens from scoring the winning touchdown during the fourth quarter of their playoff game Jan. 3, 1999, in San Francisco. The loss began a run of playoff frustration for the Packers under Favre. (above) Favre leaves the field after defeating the Denver Broncos in the final game of the season in 2003 at Lambeau Field. Also that day, Arizona upset Minnesota, gift-wrapping a playoff berth for the Packers.

when we say the team wasn't as good," Favre said. "I really don't put any added burden on myself for those losses. I felt like I played as well as I could. Obviously we didn't win the games and statistically speaking it was not enough to carry us on to the next week. But I don't think it was a reflection of my age or whatever.

"I think that's just the way it went. Some of those seasons statistically, I was as good as I was at any other time. As we know in the playoffs it comes down to one game and how you play that game; it's not how you played the previous 16 or 17. I'm not going to beat myself up over it. It is what it is."

The year that could be remembered as Favre's first best shot at getting back to the Super Bowl was '03, when the Packers squeaked into the playoffs on the final day of the season, the result of Minnesota losing on a last-second touchdown in Arizona.

It was an extension of the emotional wave Favre never imagined having to endure so late in his career. Just six days earlier, he had played the game of his life against the Oakland Raiders on "Monday Night Football," throwing for 399 yards and four touchdowns. It came a day after he learned of the death of his father, Irvin.

Given another shot at the post-season, the Packers won in overtime against Seattle in the first round and the following week took a 14-0 lead against the injury-riddled Eagles at Lincoln Financial Field. The Eagles stormed back and eventually won the game in overtime on David Akers' 31-yard field goal, advancing to play Carolina in the NFC Championship Game.

Three plays stood out in that game:

Sherman's decision to punt on fourth and 1 from the Philadelphia 41 with the Packers ahead, 17-14, and 2 minutes 30 seconds to go; the fateful "fourth-and-26" play, which occurred on the ensuing Eagles possession and allowed them to keep alive a drive that resulted in a tying field goal; and Favre's desperation heave in overtime that safety Brian Dawkins intercepted and returned 34 yards to set up the winning field goal.

Favre's poor decision in the face of a blitz will be one of the lasting memories of the game because, despite the two

Benny Sieu

FINAL YEARS TAKE A TOLL

Despite resurgence in 2007, Favre calls it a career

By Gary D'Amato

Year after year, Sunday after Sunday, Brett Favre played football with a passion and determination that was off the charts.

He outlasted head coaches Mike Holmgren, Ray Rhodes and Mike Sherman. He outlasted dozens of position coaches. He outlasted hundreds of teammates and thousands of opponents.

Then, one day, he looked around the locker room and he was nearly twice as old as the rookies. Away from the football field, he had little in common with them. Once the king of cut-ups, Favre lost a little bit of his zeal for pranks and practical jokes and Farrelly brothers humor.

He wasn't aloof, but he no longer was hanging out with the boys.

"I always enjoyed playing the game and having fun and cracking up and things like that and I didn't do that as much," he said. "I maybe was not as good a teammate from that standpoint as I once was."

For that reason and others, retirement was starting to weigh heavily on his mind. Favre wondered aloud if he was the right quarterback to lead a young team, especially in 2005, when the Packers struggled to a 4-12 record, their first losing season in 14 years.

By the quarterback's lofty standards, he had played poorly. Though he completed a career-best 372 passes, he also threw a career-high 29 interceptions and had a career-low passer rating of 70.9.

Following Green Bay's season-ending, 23-17 victory over Seattle, Favre reportedly told Holmgren, the Seahawks coach, that he was not coming back. A few weeks earlier, he had said he would be reluctant to return if Sherman wasn't the head coach because he didn't know if he had it in him to learn a new offense.

General manager Ted Thompson fired Sherman on Jan. 2, 2006, and 10 days later Mike McCarthy signed a contract to be the 16th head coach in franchise history.

All signs pointed to Favre retiring, and his months-long decision-making process left team officials and fans alike to wonder.

Finally, the week before the draft in April 2006, Favre decided to play at least one more year.

Even though McCarthy's version of the West Coast offense was nearly identical to the offense Favre had run for years, the coach used different terminology and challenged Favre to learn it. He also challenged his veteran quarterback to play more efficiently.

The results were mixed in 2006, with the Packers going 8-8 and Favre improving only marginally. He completed

Favre talks about his decision to retire at a news conference March 6, 2008, in Green Bay.

Mark Hoffman

Benny Sieu

Joe Koshollek

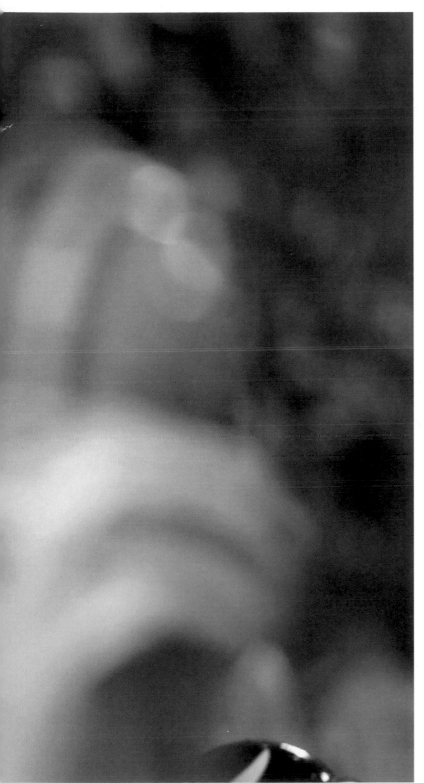

(opposite) Favre lets fly his 421st record-setting touchdown pass to Greg Jennings on Sept. 30, 2007. (top) Favre, shown here with Mike McCarthy, said he would be reluctant to continue playing after the 2005 season if coach Mike Sherman did not return. General manager Ted Thompson fired Sherman, hired McCarthy – and Favre returned. (above) Fans celebrate the record touchdown pass during the first quarter against the Vikings on Sept. 30, 2007, in Minneapolis. Favre's 421st touchdown pass eclipsed Dan Marino's record. And, the Packers won, 23-16.

just 56% of his passes, a career low, but did cut his interception total from 29 to 18.

In a tearful, on-field television interview following the Packers' 26-7 victory over the Super Bowl-bound Chicago Bears in the season finale, it sounded as if Favre had played his final game.

"What a way to go out," he said, tears filling his eyes. "Chicago's obviously a great football team. I wasn't too optimistic but here we are with a win. I couldn't ask for a better way to go out."

Said McCarthy, "It's an emotional football game and I'm sure it's emotional for him. How many more games he has left, I do not know."

Once again, Favre huddled with his family and close friends in Mississippi and weighed the pros and cons of returning. Even though he reportedly was upset that the

(opposite) Favre reacts to a third-quarter touchdown in the 42-20 "snow bowl" playoff victory over Seattle on Jan. 12, 2008, in Green Bay. The game gave fans one last beautiful remembrance of Favre's magic before his career ended the next week in a playoff loss to the Giants. (above) Sporting their Brett Favre jerseys, dejected fans sit in the frigid air after the Packers lost the NFC Championship Game to the Giants, 23-20, on Jan. 20, 2008 in Green Bay.

Jeffrey Phelps

Rick Wood

Favre hands the reins over to Aaron Rodgers in the final minutes of the playoff victory in the "snow bowl" game against Seattle on Jan. 12, 2008, at Lambeau Field.

So why, if he was still capable of playing at a high level, did he walk away? Why quit with the young Packers perhaps on the cusp of another Super Bowl? Why retire when he seemed to be having so much fun on the field?

The answer was that Favre's fun was limited to those three hours on Sunday afternoons when he was a kid again, when he butted helmets with linebackers and zinged passes between safeties and beat the blitz and taught those kids around him in the huddle how to win.

That stuff was a blast. But the rest? He grew tired of putting in all the extra hours, grew tired of watching video alone on Saturday nights at Lambeau, grew tired of the constant mental grind of preparing for next week.

He grew tired of pulling out his laptop at home and studying upcoming opponents when he could have been spending time with his wife, Deanna, and daughters, Brittany and Breleigh.

"I know I can play," Favre said. "But this year — and this is not the first year but it really to me and Deanna was more noticeable — the stress part of it. It's demanding. It

gray crept into Favre's beard and the long, numbing winters in Green Bay gave way to the promise of seasons to come, they knew this day was inevitable.

Still, it was hard – as endings often are – to accept.

In a halting, heartfelt 935-word opening statement during his retirement news conference in the appropriately named Legends Room in the Lambeau Field Atrium, Favre choked back tears and had to stop several times to compose himself.

"I've given everything I can possibly give to this organization, to the game of football, and I don't think I've got anything left to give," he said. "I know I can play, but I don't think I want to. And that's what it really comes down to. … It's been a great career for me, and it's over."

After 16 seasons with the Packers, after glorious highs and crushing lows, after 275 consecutive starts including playoffs and a record book re-written, the most famous athlete in Wisconsin sports history and one of the greatest quarterbacks of all time had thrown his final pass.

Packers fans were left not with the anticipation of Favre returning but with incandescent memories of the thrill ride that was his career. Asked to describe his most memorable play or game, Favre simply shook his head. There were so very, very many.

"I think most people who have never played football would kill to have just one play and I had thousands and thousands of plays," he said. "But the thing that is unique about me is that every one of those plays meant something to me, and I really mean that. I never took a play off."

The time went by as fast as one of Favre's bullets into double-coverage.

It hardly seemed possible that more than 15 years had elapsed since Don Majkowski suffered that fateful ankle injury against the Cincinnati Bengals and Favre came off the bench to lead a come-from-behind, 24-23 victory.

Little did Favre or anyone else know that it was the beginning of a Hall of Fame career. He would start every game for the next 16 years, lead Green Bay to 13 winning seasons and two Super Bowls, win 160 games and break every significant NFL career passing record.

Along the way, he would go from hero to icon, from respected to admired, from admired to beloved. He became one of the most famous athletes in America,

became the face of the NFL. Even the fans of opposing teams grudgingly admitted he was fun to watch.

"I think he plays the game like you would if you were in a backyard and you were wearing Wrangler jeans," Thompson said. "He loves to play the game. He loves the competition. I can't say he loves getting hit, but he's OK with it.

"He's never been a fancy-pants quarterback that doesn't like to mix it up. He likes to play the game and he appreciates the people who play the game alongside him. And I think people can relate to that."

The night before he flew from his home in Hattiesburg, Miss., to Green Bay to announce his retirement, Favre watched with amusement some of the fawning TV tributes to him and joked that he knew "what it's like to die." He could only shake his head and laugh at the naïve kid he was in the early '90s.

"It's a good thing I didn't know any better," he said. "I watch those interviews, and it's painful to watch. But in a lot of ways that was good for me. I had talent (but) probably thought I had more. I probably thought a little more of myself than I should have.

"Believe me, I knew all about the Green Bay Packers and those great players that have played here before. Knew all about the tradition. But I thought, 'What's the big deal?' If I had to go back with the same mentality right now that I have and start over, I probably wouldn't make it because I'm so much more aware of how difficult it is to win, to prepare.

"I'm well aware of the expectations. Back then it was like, 'Bring 'em on. No big deal.' That mentality helped me, as I look back. It's painful to watch, but it helped me."

Favre said the loss to the Giants in the NFC Championship Game had no bearing on his decision to retire. He also dismissed reports in which his older brother, Scott, and agent, James "Bus" Cook, were quoted as saying the Packers didn't seem to want him back.

"I know there's been some comments and issues in the press lately about why I'm leaving, whether or not the Packers did enough, whether or not Ted and Mike tried to convince me to stay," Favre said. "None of those things have anything to do with me retiring. And that's from the heart."

always has been, but I think as I've gotten older I'm much more aware of that. I'm much more aware of how hard it is to win in this league and to play at a high level. I'm not up to the challenge anymore. I can play, but I'm not up to the challenge. You can't just show up and play for three hours on Sunday. If you could, there'd be a lot more people doing it and they'd be doing it for a lot longer.

"I have way too much pride. I expect a lot out of myself and if I cannot do those things 100%, then I can't play."

In the end, it wasn't the losing that got to him, but the fear of losing. Back when he was a cocky kid who didn't know any better, the losses were a lot easier to shrug off. He had his whole career in front of him. He knew he'd win his share of games, and then some.

But in the latter years of his career, the expectations – month after month, week after week, day after day – took a heavy toll.

The more people deified him, the more uncomfortable he became in his own skin.

"Brett Favre got hard to live up to," he said. "I found myself during tough games, tough situations, other guys on the team or even Mike at times would turn to me and say, 'All right, Brett, this is where you're at your best. Pull us out.' I'm thinking, 'Ugh.' I'm thinking, 'Boy, it sure would be nice to be up about 14 right now.'

"It's just hard. It got hard. I did it, but it's hard. And I don't think it would get easier next year or the following year. It's only gotten tougher and something told me, 'It's gotten too hard for you.' "

So he walked away. He agonized for weeks over the decision and even as he said the words "I'm retiring" he couldn't be 100% certain he was doing the right thing. He knew he would miss the game, miss the camaraderie, miss those Sunday afternoons when he stood under center at Lambeau Field and 70,000 people were screaming at the top of their lungs and there, down the sideline, he saw a receiver breaking free …

"Will I find something to do that's equal to throwing a touchdown pass at Lambeau Field? I doubt it," Favre said. "Will I find something equal to playing in the Super Bowl? I doubt it. I'm not even going to try.

"There really isn't a plan. I know this place and what it's meant to my career is really special, and to think that I can

find something to replace that and feel the same … I'm no fool. I know there's nothing out there like that."

And so the Packers moved forward with Aaron Rodgers, the team's first-round draft pick in 2005. Thompson and McCarthy were high on Rodgers' potential, but going into the 2008 season he had little game experience and questionable durability.

"I wish Aaron the best of luck," Favre said. "I think he'll do a fine job. I know everyone's made comments that, boy, (he's got) big shoes to fill. The only shoes he has to fill are his. He doesn't need to play like Brett Favre. It's all about the cast around you; it's all about the coaching staff.

"If you stay focused on the fact that it's not about you – they obviously drafted him because he has the talent and mental capabilities – he'll be fine. Hopefully, one day he's sitting here where I am and able to experience what I have been able to experience."

As for Favre, he won't be hanging around Green Bay, regaling anybody who will listen about that pass he threw to Andre Rison in Super Bowl XXXI. No offense to Fuzzy Thurston or Jerry Kramer, but that's not his style.

Nor will Favre be joining Terry Bradshaw in the studio or Troy Aikman in the broadcast booth. He planned to keep a low profile; Deanna said for at least one year they would pull back from their public appearances and events.

"The last thing I want to be is one of those guys who hangs around and, because of my status, they keep me around, they don't know how to tell me no," Favre said. "Will I be a Green Bay Packer for life? Sure. That doesn't mean I come in and give my opinions and things like that."

What will he do? Favre said he planned to take Deanna's advice and look at life through the windshield instead of the rear-view mirror. So he's looking forward to doing … what, exactly?

"Nothing," he said.

"Ron Wolf asked me, 'What are you going to do?' I said, 'Nothing.' And I'm going to stick to that until I want to do something else." ❹

Favre walks out of the locker room
with his teammates before making
his 250th straight regular-season start
against the Oakland Raiders on Dec.
9, 2007 at Lambeau Field. The
Packers won 38-7.

7

Benny Sieu; next page: Jeffrey Phelps

THE COMPETITOR
The love of the battle motivated Favre

(left) Tampa Bay defensive tackle Warren Sapp was one of several intense defensive linemen – others included Minnesota's yapping John Randle and the Giants' Michael Strahan – with whom Favre had a love/hate relationship. Favre had tremendous respect for the intensity of their play and often could be seen joking with them, sometimes right after they had planted him in the turf. Sapp retired on the same day as Favre. (above) Favre runs full tilt as he outdistances fullback William Henderson during wind sprints in the Don Hutson Center, one of the Packer practice facilities, in 1999. "We shouldn't have done that," an exhausted Favre said to Henderson when they finally slowed down to catch their breath.

MILLER TIME

PENSKE
Truck Rental

WE RENT
TRUCKS

...ds to Go
Ball On
1 Quarter

15:00

For Brett Favre, nothing could compare to the three magical hours on Sunday when he and his teammates were able to match their skills against those of their opponents. Favre always said the huge amount of money he was paid was the icing on the cake. By their reaction, fans at perpetually sold-out Lambeau Field showed that they believed him.

Receiver Robert Brooks hurdles Favre, who was blocking the Baltimore Ravens' DeRon Jenkins on a reverse in October 1998 at Lambeau Field. The Packers won, 28-10. Favre took pride in not being a "pretty boy" quarterback and was not afraid to lay out for his teammates. He always said that though he was a quarterback, he had a lineman's mentality.

(left)
Q. Why did the quarterback fall backward?
A. Because he wanted to throw an 80-yard touchdown.

The details: Favre to Greg Jennings during a 38-7 victory
over Oakland in December 2007 at Lambeau Field.

(above) To the uninitiated, this might look like Favre
playing "itsy-bitsy" spider. He is calling an audible at
the line of scrimmage in a 34-13 home victory over
Detroit in December 2007.

previous page: Benny Sieu; (above) Rick Wood

BELOVED BY ALL

In an era of me-first athletes, Favre earned the respect of fans, foes, teammates and the media with his everyman, working-class approach to his job

(opposite) The Atlanta Falcons' DeAngelo Hall and his son watch Favre sign his old Falcons jersey for the son after the Packers' 33-25 victory over Atlanta on Nov. 13, 2005, in Atlanta.

(left) Favre leaps into the arms of center Mike Flanagan after throwing a touchdown pass to Antonio Chatman against Seattle in January 2006 in Green Bay.

ONE MORE !!!

In the last years of Favre's career, the "tractor watch" became a ritual during the frigid days of the Midwestern winter. Will Brett be back? Or will he retire to his lawn tractor? The pleas of these fans at the Seattle game on New Year's Day 2006 were rewarded for two more seasons before Favre retired in March 2008.

Karen Sherlock

(above) If you can't get his written autograph, what's the next best thing?
Three Marine lance corporals from Wisconsin, Jayson Wissmueller (left), of Grafton;
Joseph Stewart, of South Milwaukee; and Matthew Bannach, of Franklin,
display their creative answer: tattoos of Favre's signature. They are shown during training
in 2007 at the Marine Corps Air Ground Combat Center in Twentynine Palms, Calif.

(opposite) Back in the day when his signature could still be obtained, Favre wades through a sea
of autograph seekers in 1994 during training camp in Green Bay.

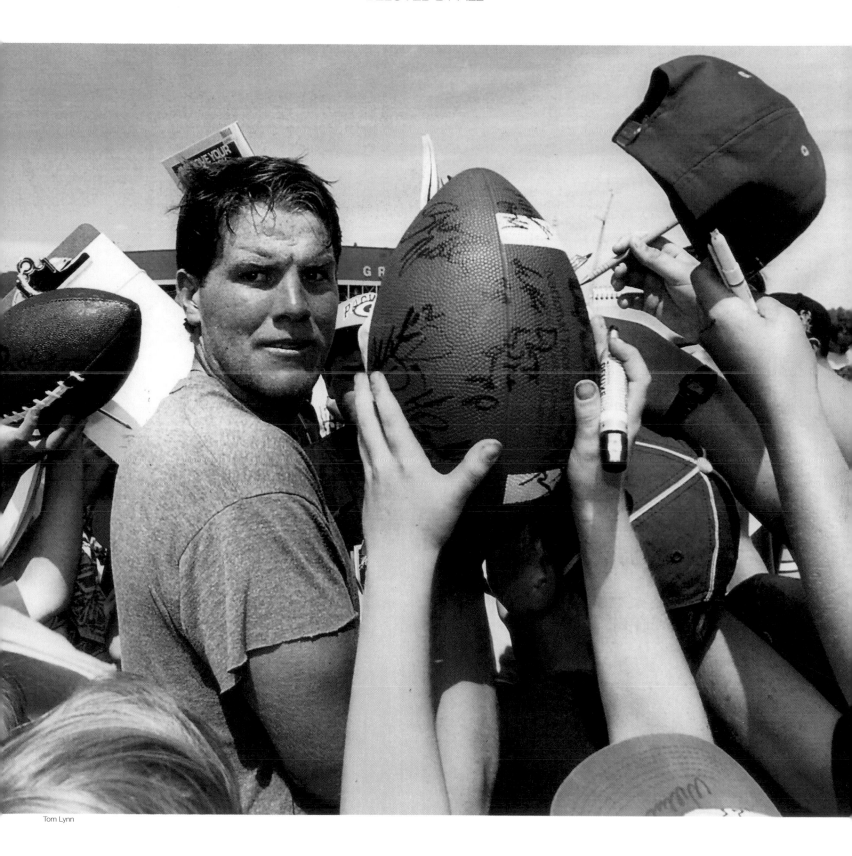

Tom Lynn

Gary Porter

(above) Favre shares a playful moment with teammate Antonio Freeman after a victory over Tampa Bay in November, 2001. Freeman caught more touchdown passes from Favre than any other Packer, and the respect they have for each other continues on into their retirements.

(opposite) Favre is one of few NFL players who can say they didn't retire until one of his children was in college. Here he and wife Deanna and daughters Breleigh and Brittany (a college freshman) walk off the field after the Packers defeated Seattle in the "snow bowl" playoff game Jan. 12, 2008, at Lambeau Field. Favre's last game turned out to be the following week, a loss to the New York Giants in the NFC Championship Game.

Rick Wood

David Joles

David Joles

Rick Wood

HAVING A BALL

If it's round and soars through the air, Favre is there – and often, for charity

Tom Lynn

(opposite) Favre makes a throw during a Packers charity softball game in 2002 in Grand Chute, Wis. The proceeds from the game, which pitted the Packers offense vs. the defense, benefited the Brett Favre Fourward Foundation, whose mission is to provide aid to disadvantaged or disabled children in Wisconsin.

(top left) Favre does some tongue-wagging while taking batting practice before a Milwaukee Brewers game at Milwaukee County Stadium in 1998.

(above) Favre at the U.S. Bank Championship Charity Shootout in Milwaukee in July 2005. Favre teamed with PGA pro Jerry Kelly of Madison, Wis., to win $20,000 for the Brett Favre Fourward Foundation.

(left) The ever-spontaneous Favre throws a snowball at teammate Donald Driver to celebrate a touchdown in the 42-20 "snow bowl" playoff victory over Seattle on Jan. 12, 2008, in Green Bay.

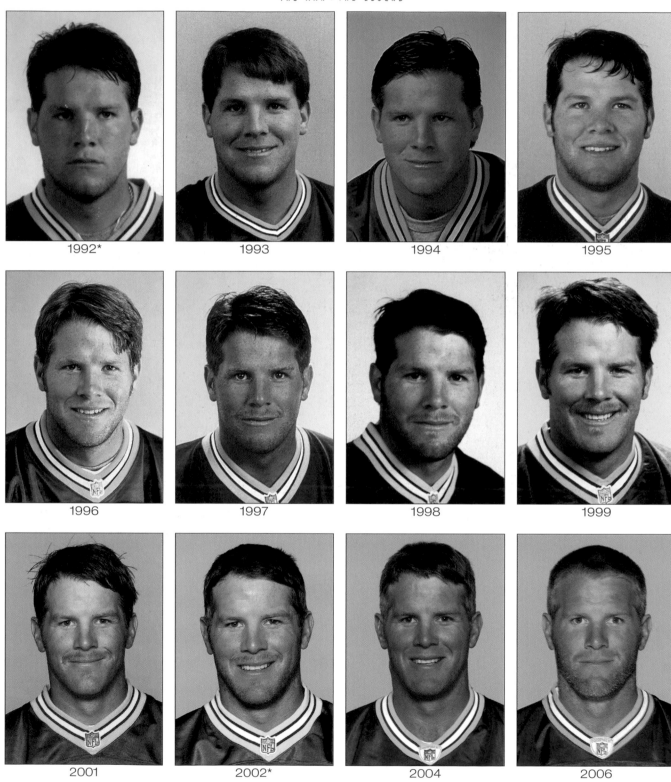

1992*   1993   1994   1995

1996   1997   1998   1999

2001   2002*   2004   2006

Karen Sherlock

ONE MAGIC MOMENT

Favre's miracle encounter with a burn survivor
By Bob Friday

Howard Ross was burned over 75% of his body as a child. In 1998, he and two other Children's Champions from Children's Hospital in Milwaukee attended a Milwaukee Wave soccer game as part of a One on One With Brett Favre.

Howard walked with his crutches toward Favre. Then Favre asked him about his crutches. "Do you need these, son?" Favre said. "I guess not," Howard replied.

Favre took the crutches, held them in the air and backed away. Howard hiked the ball to Brett, Favre threw a pass and then backed away, saying, "Come over here, Howard."

At age 8 and after spending almost a year at Children's Hospital, Howard took his first steps since being burned by walking into Favre's arms. The crowd erupted.

Howard, now Howard Nolan, went on to play football, basketball and baseball at Dominican High School in Whitefish Bay, Wis. He will graduate in 2009.

(opposite) From young pup to grizzled veteran: The maturation of a future Hall of Famer.

Official team photos
*No photo taken for 2000, 2003, 2005, 2007

Favre's year-by-year statistics

1991   With Atlanta Falcons

G	ATT.	COMP.	PCT.	YDS.	TD	INT.
2	4	0	0.0	0	0	2

1992   9-7   Failed to make playoffs

G	ATT.	COMP.	PCT.	YDS.	TD	INT.
15	471	302	64.1	3,227	18	13

Brett Favre takes over the starting quarterback job in the fourth game of the season against the Pittsburgh Steelers.

1993   9-7   Wild Card

G	ATT.	COMP.	PCT.	YDS.	TD	INT.
16	522	318	60.9	3,303	19	24

Packers fall to the eventual Super Bowl champion Dallas Cowboys in the playoffs.

1994   9-7   Wild Card

G	ATT.	COMP.	PCT.	YDS.	TD	INT.
16	582	363	62.4	3,882	33	14

The Cowboys once again ended Green Bay's playoff run with a 35-9 drubbing.

1995   11-5   NFC Central champs

G	ATT.	COMP.	PCT.	YDS.	TD	INT.
16	570	359	63.0	4,413	38	13

Green Bay earned its first NFC Central title in 23 years with a 24-19 victory over Pittsburgh before losing to Dallas in the NFC Championship Game.

1996   13-3   NFC Central champs

G	ATT.	COMP.	PCT.	YDS.	TD	INT.
16	543	325	59.9	3,899	39	13

Beat the New England Patriots 35-21 in Super Bowl XXXI. Favre had two touchdown passes and zero interceptions.

1997   13-3   NFC Central champs

G	ATT.	COMP.	PCT.	YDS.	TD	INT.
16	513	304	59.3	3,867	35	16

Back in the Super Bowl for the second straight year, the Packers lost to the Denver Broncos, 31-24.

1998   11-5   Wild Card

G	ATT.	COMP.	PCT.	YDS.	TD	INT.
16	551	347	63.0	4,212	31	23

Lost a wild-card matchup with the San Francisco 49ers in the closing seconds of the game. Head coach Mike Holmgren leaves the Packers.

1999   8-8   Failed to make playoffs

G	ATT.	COMP.	PCT.	YDS.	TD	INT.
16	595	341	57.3	4,091	22	23

Packers miss playoffs for the first time in six years, under the helm of first-year head coach Ray Rhodes.

2000   9-7   Failed to make playoffs

G	ATT.	COMP.	PCT.	YDS.	TD	INT.
16	580	338	58.3	3,812	20	16

Mike Sherman takes over as head coach and misses the playoffs again.

2001   12-4   Wild Card

G	ATT.	COMP.	PCT.	YDS.	TD	INT.
16	510	314	61.6	3,921	32	15

Season ends on a six-interception performance by Favre against St. Louis in the playoffs.

2002   12-4   NFC North champs

G	ATT.	COMP.	PCT.	YDS.	TD	INT.
16	551	341	61.9	3,658	27	16

The Packers finished the regular season an undefeated 8-0 at home. Lost to Atlanta at home in the playoffs.

2003   10-6   NFC North champs

G	ATT.	COMP.	PCT.	YDS.	TD	INT.
16	471	308	65.4	3,361	32	21

Lost in the playoffs on the "4th and 26" play against the Philadelphia Eagles. Favre finished the regular season with the most touchdown passes (32) in the league for the fourth time in his career.

2004   10-6   NFC North champs

G	ATT.	COMP.	PCT.	YDS.	TD	INT.
16	540	346	64.1	4,088	30	17

The Packers rallied from losing four of their first five games to still make the playoffs. Lost to Minnesota at home in the playoffs.

2005   4-12   Failed to make playoffs

G	ATT.	COMP.	PCT.	YDS.	TD	INT.
16	607	372	61.3	3,881	20	29

Green Bay's first losing record since Favre took over at quarterback.

2006   8-8   Failed to make playoffs

G	ATT.	COMP.	PCT.	YDS.	TD	INT.
16	613	343	56.0	3,885	18	18

Packers miss the playoffs, but win final four games of the season.

2007   13-3   NFC North champs

G	ATT.	COMP.	PCT.	YDS.	TD	INT.
16	535	356	66.5	4,155	28	15

Packers surprise everyone, winning the division before losing in the NFC Championship Game to the New York Giants at home.

NFL totals   17 seasons

G	ATT.	COMP.	PCT.	YDS.	TD	INT.
257	8,758	5,377	61.4	61,655	442	288

Favre's playoff statistics

1993

GP	ATT.	COMP.	PCT.	YDS.	TD	INT.
2	71	43	60.6	535	5	3

1994

GP	ATT.	COMP.	PCT.	YDS.	TD	INT.
2	73	41	56.2	473	0	1

1995

GP	ATT.	COMP.	PCT.	YDS.	TD	INT.
3	102	66	64.7	805	8	2

1996

GP	ATT.	COMP.	PCT.	YDS.	TD	INT.
3	71	44	62.0	617	5	1

1997

GP	ATT.	COMP.	PCT.	YDS.	TD	INT.
3	97	56	57.7	668	5	3

1998

GP	ATT.	COMP.	PCT.	YDS.	TD	INT.
1	35	20	57.1	292	2	2

2001

GP	ATT.	COMP.	PCT.	YDS.	TD	INT.
2	73	48	65.8	550	4	7

2002

GP	ATT.	COMP.	PCT.	YDS.	TD	INT.
1	42	20	47.6	247	1	2

2003

GP	ATT.	COMP.	PCT.	YDS.	TD	INT.
2	66	41	62.1	499	3	1

2004

GP	ATT.	COMP.	PCT.	YDS.	TD	INT.
1	33	22	66.7	216	1	4

2007

GP	ATT.	COMP.	PCT.	YDS.	TD	INT.
2	37	58	63.8	409	5	2

Playoffs totals

GP	ATT.	COMP.	PCT.	YDS.	TD	INT.
22	449	710	63.2	5,311	39	28

Favre victories, by stadium

STADIUM	W	L	PCT.
Lambeau Field, Green Bay	89	28	.761
Soldier Field, Chicago	12	3	.800
Milwaukee County Stadium	7	2	.778
HHH Metrodome, Minneapolis	6	10	.375
Houlihan's/Tampa Stadium	4	1	.800
Bank of America/Ericsson Stadium, Charlotte	4	2	.667
Ford Field, Detroit	4	2	.667
Monster/3Com Park, San Francisco	3	0	1.000
Qualcomm/Jack Murphy Stadium, San Diego	3	0	1.000
Giants Stadium, East Rutherford, N.J.	3	2	.600
Pontiac Silverdome	3	7	.300
ALLTEL Stadium, Jacksonville, Fla.	2	0	1.000
Edward Jones/Trans World Dome, St. Louis	2	1	.667
Louisiana Superdome	2	1	.667
Astrodome, Houston	1	0	1.000
Cinergy Field/Riverfront Stadium, Cincinnati	1	0	1.000
FedEx Field, Landover, Md.	1	0	1.000
Gillette Stadium, Foxboro, Mass.	1	0	1.000
Invesco Field at Mile High, Denver	1	0	1.000
Kingdome, Seattle	1	0	1.000
Memorial Stadium, Champaign, Ill.	1	0	1.000
*Network Associates Coliseum, Oakland	1	0	1.000
Reliant Stadium, Houston	1	0	1.000
Cleveland Municipal Stadium	1	1	.500
Foxboro Stadium	1	1	.500
Georgia Dome, Atlanta	1	1	.500
Pro Player/Dolphin Stadium, Miami	1	1	.500
Sun Devil Stadium, Tempe, Ariz.	1	1	.500
Arrowhead Stadium, Kansas City	1	2	.333
Raymond Jones Stadium, Tampa, Fla.	1	5	.167
Fulton County Stadium, Atlanta	0	0	—
RFK Stadium, Washington	0	0	—
*The Coliseum/Adelphia Coliseum, Nashville	0	1	.000
M & T Bank Stadium, Baltimore	0	1	.000
Mile High Stadium, Denver	0	1	.000
Paul Brown Stadium, Cincinnati	0	1	.000
Qwest Field, Seattle	0	1	.000
Three Rivers Stadium, Pittsburgh	0	1	.000
RCA Dome, Indianapolis	0	2	.000
Veterans Stadium, Philadelphia	0	2	.000
Lincoln Financial Field, Philadelphia	0	3	.000
Ralph Wilson/Rich Stadium, Buffalo	0	3	.000
Texas Stadium, Irving	0	6	.000
Career Totals	**160**	**93**	**.632**

* The Coliseum became LP Field and Network Associates Coliseum became McAfee Coliseum before the 2006 season.

Favre TD passes, by stadium   (regular season only)

TD	STADIUM
209	Lambeau Field, Green Bay
25	Soldier Field, Chicago
24	HHH Metrodome, Minneapolis
17	Bank of America/Ericsson Stadium, Charlotte
17	Milwaukee County Stadium
15	Pontiac Silverdome
14	Houlihan's/Tampa Stadium
13	Ford Field, Detroit
8	Giants Stadium, East Rutherford
7	Louisiana Superdome
7	Qualcomm/Jack Murphy Stadium, San Diego
7	RCA Dome, Indianapolis
7	Texas Stadium, Irving
6	Edward Jones/Trans World Dome, St. Louis
6	Ralph Wilson/Rich Stadium, Buffalo
6	Raymond James Stadium, Tampa, Fla.
5	ALLTEL Stadium, Jacksonville, Fla.
5	Arrowhead Stadium, Kansas City
5	Monster/3Com Park, San Francisco

TD	STADIUM
4	Foxboro Stadium
4	Kingdome, Seattle
4	*Network Associates Coliseum, Oakland
3	Cleveland Municipal Stadium
3	Gillette Stadium, Foxboro, Mass.
3	Memorial Stadium, Champaign, Ill.
2	*The Coliseum/Adelphia Coliseum, Nashville
2	Dolphin/Pro Player Stadium, Miami
2	Georgia Dome, Atlanta
2	Invesco Field at Mile High, Denver
2	Sun Devil Stadium, Tempe, Ari.
1	Astrodome, Houston
1	Cinergy Field/Riverfront Stadium, Cincinnati
1	FedEx Field, Landover, Md.
1	Lincoln Financial Field, Philadelphia
1	Paul Brown Stadium, Cincinnati
1	Qwest Field, Seattle
1	Reliant Stadium, Houston
1	Veterans Stadium, Philadelphia
442	**Career Totals**

* The Coliseum became LP Field and Network Associates Coliseum became McAfee Coliseum before the 2006 season.

Favre's salaries

YEAR	BASE SALARY	BONUSES
1991	$260,000	$450,000 signing bonus (three years, $1.43 million)
1992	$310,000	$25,000 roster bonus
1993	$360,000	$25,000 roster bonus
1994	$1.6 million	$2.5 million signing bonus, $500,000 reporting bonus (5 years, $19 million; July 14)
1995	$2.9 million	
1996	$3.6 million	
1997	$1.6 million	$12 million signing bonus** (seven years, $47.25 million; July 26-27)
1998	$3.1 million	
1999	$4.3 million	
2000	$5.35 million	
2001	$477,000	$11 million signing bonus (10 years, $101.5 million; March 1)
2002	$723,000	$4 million roster bonus.
2003	$4.3 million	$3 million roster bonus.
2004	$5.5 million	$3 million roster bonus.
2005	$6.5 million	$3 million roster bonus.
2006	$7 million	$3 million roster bonus.
2007	$11 million	

$101.38 million

* Contract signed with Atlanta Falcons ($450,000 signing bonus, base salaries unavailable)

**Signing bonus paid in equal parts over a three-year period.

Career injuries

INJURY	SUFFERED	FIRST GAME BACK	RESULT
First-degree separation, left shoulder	vs. Philadelphia, Nov. 15, 1992	at Chicago, Nov. 22, 1992	W
Deep thigh bruise	vs. Tampa Bay, Nov. 28, 1993	at Chicago, Dec. 5, 1993	L
Severely bruised left hip	at Minnesota, Oct. 20, 1994	at Chicago, Oct. 31, 1994	W
Severely sprained left ankle	at Minnesota, Nov. 5, 1995	vs. Chicago, Nov. 12, 1995	W
Wind knocked out (twice)	vs. Pittsburgh, Dec. 24, 1995	vs. Atlanta, Dec. 31, 1995	W
Sprained thumb, right hand	vs. Denver, Aug. 23, 1999	vs. Oakland, Sept. 12, 1999	W
Tendinitis, right elbow	training camp	vs. New York Jets, Sept. 3, 2000	L
Left mid-foot sprain	at Tampa Bay, Nov. 12, 2000	vs. Indianapolis, Nov.19, 2000	W
Sprained lateral collateral ligament, left knee	vs. Washington, Oct. 20, 2002	vs. Miami, Nov. 4, 2002	W
Broken thumb, right hand	at St. Louis, Oct 19, 2003	at Minnesota, Nov. 2, 2003	W
Softball-sized bruise, left hamstring	at Indianapolis, Sept. 26, 2004	vs. New York Giants, Oct. 3, 2004	L
Concussion	vs. N.Y. Giants, Oct. 3, 2004	vs. Tennessee, Oct. 11, 2004	L
Sprained right hand	vs. Dallas, Oct 24, 2004	at Washington, Oct. 31, 2004	W
Ankle	at Tennessee, Sept. 1, 2005	at Dallas, Sept. 11, 2005	L
Ulnar nerve, right elbow	vs. New England, Nov. 19, 2006	at Seattle, Nov. 27, 2006	L
Right elbow, left shoulder	at Dallas, Nov. 29, 2007	vs. Oakland, Dec. 9, 2007	W

Passing yards
Record broken: Dec. 16, 2007, at St. Louis

IN THOUSANDS

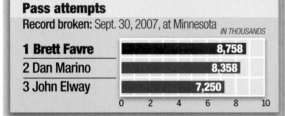

1 Brett Favre	61,655
2 Dan Marino	61,361
3 John Elway	51,475

0 20 40 60 80

Pass attempts
Record broken: Sept. 30, 2007, at Minnesota

IN THOUSANDS

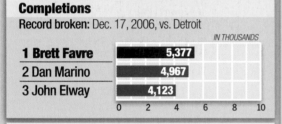

1 Brett Favre	8,758
2 Dan Marino	8,358
3 John Elway	7,250

0 2 4 6 8 10

Completions
Record broken: Dec. 17, 2006, vs. Detroit

IN THOUSANDS

1 Brett Favre	5,377
2 Dan Marino	4,967
3 John Elway	4,123

0 2 4 6 8 10

Touchdown passes
Record broken: Sept. 30, 2007, at Minnesota

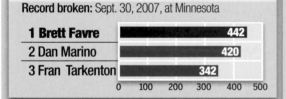

1 Brett Favre	442
2 Dan Marino	420
3 Fran Tarkenton	342

0 100 200 300 400 500

Victories by quarterback
Record broken: Sept. 16, 2007, at New York Giants

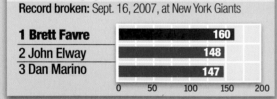

1 Brett Favre	160
2 John Elway	148
3 Dan Marino	147

0 50 100 150 200

Interceptions
Record broken: Oct. 14, 2007, vs. Washington

1 Brett Favre	288
2 George Blanda	277
3 John Hadl	268

0 100 200 300 400

Top targets
Here are the 44 players who have caught TD passes from Favre, along with the number caught by each player.

Antonio Freeman	57
Sterling Sharpe	41
Donald Driver	36
Robert Brooks	32
Bubba Franks	29
Bill Schroeder	19
Javon Walker	19
Mark Chmura	16
Dorsey Levens	16
Greg Jennings	15
Ahman Green	14
William Henderson	13
Tyrone Davis	12
Robert Ferguson	12
Keith Jackson	11
Edgar Bennett	10
David Martin	9
Donald Lee	8
Anthony Morgan	8
Corey Bradford	7
Jackie Harris	6
Antonio Chatman	5
Tony Fisher	5
Derrick Mayes	5
Ruvell Martin	4
Don Beebe	4
Mark Clayton	3
Mark Ingram	3
Terry Mickens	3
James Jones	2
Terry Glenn	2
Noah Herron	2
Charles Jordan	2
Jeff Thomason	2
Ed West	2
Koren Robinson	1
Reggie Cobb	1
Samkon Gado	1
Charles Lee	1
Andre Rison	1
Harry Sydney	1
Kitrick Taylor	1
Darrell Thompson	1
Wesley Walls	1

Favre's 39 comeback victories

DATE	OPPONENT	SCORE	SCORING PLAY
Sept. 20, 1992	vs. Cincinnati	24-23	35-yd. pass to Kitrick Taylor
Nov. 15, 1992	vs. Philadelphia	27-24	Chris Jacke 41-yd. FG
Nov. 29, 1992	vs. Tampa Bay	19-14	9-yd. pass to Jackie Harris
Nov. 14, 1993	at New Orleans	19-17	Jacke 36-yd. FG
Nov. 21, 1993	vs. Detroit	26-17	Jacke 34-yd. FG
Nov. 28, 1993	vs. Tampa Bay	13-10	2-yd. pass to Sterling Sharpe
Jan. 8, 1994	at Detroit	28-24	40-yd. pass to Sharpe
Oct. 9, 1994	vs. L.A. Rams	24-17	Edgar Bennett 1-yd. run
Dec. 18, 1994	vs. Atlanta	21-17	Favre 9-yd run
Nov. 12, 1995	vs. Chicago	35-28	16-yd. pass to Bennett
Oct. 14, 1996	vs. San Fran.	23-20	Jacke 53-yd. FG
Nov. 1, 1998	vs. San Fran.	36-22	62-yd. pass to Antonio Freeman
Dec. 27, 1998	at Chicago	16-13	Longwell 18-yd FG
Sept. 12, 1999	vs. Oakland	28-24	1-yd. pass to Jeff Thomason
Sept. 26, 1999	vs. Minnesota	23-20	23-yd. pass to Corey Bradford
Oct. 10, 1999	vs. Tampa Bay	26-23	21-yd. pass to Freeman
Sept. 17, 2000	vs. Philadelphia	6-3	Longwell 38-yd. FG
Oct. 15, 2000	vs. San Fran.	31-28	Longwell 35-yd. FG
Nov. 6, 2000	vs. Minnesota	26-20	43-yd. pass to Freeman
Dec. 24, 2000	vs. Tampa Bay	17-14	Longwell 22-yd. FG
Dec. 3, 2001	at Jacksonville	28-21	Favre 6-yd. run
Dec. 30, 2001	vs. Minnesota	24-13	Ahman Green 4-yd. run
Jan. 13, 2002	vs. San Fran.	25-15	Longwell 45-yd. FG
Sept. 8, 2002	vs. Atlanta	37-34	Longwell 34-yd. FG
Sept. 29, 2002	vs. Carolina	17-14	22-yd. pass to Donald Driver
Dec. 8, 2002	vs. Minnesota	26-22	Tony Fisher 14-yd. run
Nov. 2, 2003	at Minnesota	30-27	12-yd. pass to Javon Walker
Nov. 16, 2003	at Tampa Bay	20-13	Green 1-yd. run
Dec. 14, 2003	at San Diego	38-21	40-yd pass to Robert Ferguson
Jan. 4, 2004	vs. Seattle	33-27	Green 1-yd. run
Nov. 14, 2004	vs. Minnesota	34-31	Longwell 33-yd. FG
Nov. 21, 2004	at Houston	16-13	Longwell 46-yd. FG
Dec. 12, 2004	vs. Detroit	16-13	Longwell 23-yd. FG
Dec. 24, 2004	at Minnesota	34-31	Longwell 29-yd. FG
Dec. 11, 2005	vs. Detroit	16-13	Longwell 28-yd. FG
Dec. 21, 2006	vs. Minnesota	9-7	Dave Rayner 44-yd. FG
Sept. 9, 2007	vs. Philadelphia	16-13	Mason Crosby 42-yd. FG
Sept. 23, 2007	vs. San Diego	31-24	57-yd. pass to Greg Jennings
Oct. 29, 2007	vs. Denver	19-13	82-yd. pass to Jennings

TDs against other teams

Team	No.	Team	No.	Team	No.	Team	No.
Vikings	54	Saints	13	Seahawks	9	Chiefs	7
Lions	54	49ers	12	Falcons	8	Cardinals	5
Bears	53	Eagles	12	Titans (Oilers)	8	Ravens	5
Buccaneers	37	Raiders	11	Broncos	8	Jets	5
Panthers	23	Giants	10	Bengals	7	Redskins	4
Rams	18	Bills	9	Dolphins	7	Steelers	4
Chargers	13	Browns	9	Jaguars	7	Texans	1
Cowboys	13	Colts	9	Patriots	7		

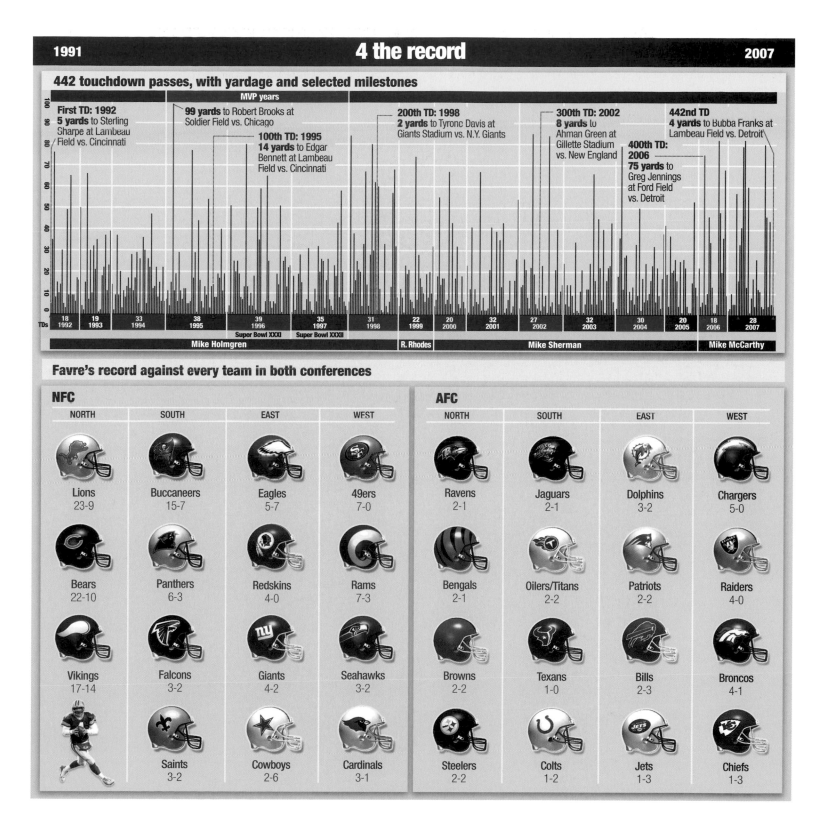

4 the record

1991 — 2007

442 touchdown passes, with yardage and selected milestones

First TD: 1992
5 yards to Sterling Sharpe at Lambeau Field vs. Cincinnati

99 yards to Robert Brooks at Soldier Field vs. Chicago

100th TD: 1995
14 yards to Edgar Bennett at Lambeau Field vs. Cincinnati

200th TD: 1998
2 yards to Tyrone Davis at Giants Stadium vs. N.Y. Giants

300th TD: 2002
8 yards to Ahman Green at Gillette Stadium vs. New England

400th TD: 2006
75 yards to Greg Jennings at Ford Field vs. Detroit

442nd TD
4 yards to Bubba Franks at Lambeau Field vs. Detroit

MVP years

TDs	18	19	33	38	39	35	31	22	20	32	27	32	30	20	18	28
	1992	1993	1994	1995	1996	1997	1998	1999	2000	2001	2002	2003	2004	2005	2006	2007

Super Bowl XXXI · Super Bowl XXXII

Mike Holmgren · R. Rhodes · Mike Sherman · Mike McCarthy

Favre's record against every team in both conferences

NFC

NORTH	SOUTH	EAST	WEST
Lions 23-9	Buccaneers 15-7	Eagles 5-7	49ers 7-0
Bears 22-10	Panthers 6-3	Redskins 4-0	Rams 7-3
Vikings 17-14	Falcons 3-2	Giants 4-2	Seahawks 3-2
	Saints 3-2	Cowboys 2-6	Cardinals 3-1

AFC

NORTH	SOUTH	EAST	WEST
Ravens 2-1	Jaguars 2-1	Dolphins 3-2	Chargers 5-0
Bengals 2-1	Oilers/Titans 2-2	Patriots 2-2	Raiders 4-0
Browns 2-2	Texans 1-0	Bills 2-3	Broncos 4-1
Steelers 2-2	Colts 1-2	Jets 1-3	Chiefs 1-3

AFTERWORD
It all started with Kitrick Taylor
By Bob Friday

Kitrick Taylor caught one touchdown pass in his six-year National Football League career – the first game-winner ever thrown by Brett Favre.

Taylor was released by the Packers in Week 11 of that 1992 season, and has not spoken with Favre since. But Taylor remembers the play from Sept. 20 of that year as that "little shot I did get on the field" that made him a part of NFL history.

The Packers started the final drive at their own 8-yard line with 1:07 remaining in the game after a field goal gave the Cincinnati Bengals a 23-17 lead. Wide receivers coach Sherman Lewis summoned Taylor, who had been picked up as a Plan B free agent by the Packers in February 1992.

"When Sterling went down, I knew I had to be the one to come back him up," Taylor said. "He was in a lot of pain."

The play that turned out to be the game-winner started with 19 seconds left from the Bengals' 35-yard line. It called for all receivers to run a 'go' route – sprint toward the end zone in specified areas.

The Bengals were playing a "Cover 2" defense, and Taylor said he knew the safeties would cheat toward tight end Jackie Harris, who lined up in the slot on the right side with Taylor.

"I told myself, 'Be ready...stay between the numbers and the sideline.'

"The corner never got a hand on me; it just opened the gates for me. I looked at the safety. He was pretty far over and I said, 'Oh goodness, it's got to come to me.'

"Brett kind of pump-faked a bit. I was wide open. I looked up and...I lost it for a split second in the glare." But then, he said, "It just fell right into the bread basket. I cradled it in and that was it. He roped it in there pretty good, over the safety.

"As I was going back to the sideline, we embraced.

"It was the greatest moment of my career."

Taylor, 43, is an administrator for group homes for teenage boys.

"I love giving back to young boys." he said. "I always feel there is hope for young boys who lack the beginning that most boys do. I want to show them that there is hope."

Very occasionally, that involves mentioning his little moment in NFL history.

"I bring it out when there is the necessity, but most of the time they find out anyway," Taylor said.

Taylor is an elder at a Church of God in Christ, and lives in Moreno Valley, Calif., with his wife, Donita, and their children.

He has followed Favre's career, and took special delight in watching Favre's pass to Greg Jennings in the 2007 season that gave Favre the record for career touchdown passes. That play, he said, "brought back a quick memory of what happened in 1992."

Favre's career didn't surprise Taylor, because Favre showed exceptional talent even in practice on the scout team running an opponent's offense.

"He would throw passes in places where I would never imagine any quarterback would throw it to," Taylor said. "I never caught a pass that came at me that precise."

And those stories about Favre's fastballs? True, Taylor said.

"He broke one of my pinkies" in practice one day, Taylor said.